BREATHE!!
Your Life Depends On It!

A to Z Guide to
Your Intuition

Pamela Storrs

Seer, Listener, Medium

D0839139

BREATHE!! Your Life Depends On It!
A to Z Guide to Your Intuition

By Pamela Storrs

Copyright 2011 Pamela Storrs

Published by Winston Words Publishing
www.WinstonWordsPublishing.com

ISBN: 978-0-9828079-0-3

DEDICATION

This book is dedicated with unconditional love to Mom.

ACKNOWLEDGEMENTS

To all who have touched my life in any fashion, thank you! This revised edition contains important exercises and passages which were either corrected or left out of the first edition; hence the self-publishing of this copy. Thank you for taking the time to reread (or read it for the first time); I know you'll find it worthwhile!

Special thanks and love to my husband Jim for your patience, inspiration, support and love (and all those details you've tended to!).

Many thanks to my birth family for being in my life. I appreciate your love and individuality! Thanks to my soul family; you know who you are! I'm glad we made it around this time; let's continue to do what we can for each other and the world!

To my friends and my clients who continue to give me loving support and are continually inspiring, I thank you. You know who you are!

To all the deceased ... it is easier to hear from you than all the rest. Thanks for the continual flow of unconditional love and wisdom; it is because of you this book was born.

Joyfully, I thank you whether I have been momentarily inspired to great heights, to laughter, or to grief. I have learned about Life and about Self from all of you who have crossed my path, whether living here or living beyond. It has all been part of this magnificent journey, and I wouldn't trade a moment of it!

BREATHE!!
Your Life Depends On It!

A to Z Guide
To Your Intuition

INTRODUCTION

AAA's
AFFIRMATIONS, ATTITUDE, AWARENESS, ALIGNMENT, ANGELS, AURAS

BBB's
BREATH & BREATHING, BALANCE, BUSI-NESS, BEING

CCC's
CLARITY, CLEARING & CLEANSING, CHANNELING, CLAIRS, CRYSTALS

DDD's
DIMENSIONS, DEATH, DREAMS

EEE's
EMPATHS, ENERGY, EXPERIENCE

FFF's
FUN, FEAR, FAMILY (AND OTHER STRANGE ENTITIES), FORGIVENESS, FREE WILL

GGG's
GIVING, GRATITUDE, GUIDES, GUILT, GODDESS/GOD/GREAT SPIRIT

HHH's
HAPPINESS, HEALTH, HEALING, HYPNOTHERAPY

III's
INTENTION, IJK, INTUITION, IMAGINATION

JJJ's
JOY, JUDGMENT, JUST DO IT!

KKK's
KINDNESS, KIDS, KNOWLEDGE

LLL's
LOVE, LAUGH, LIVE, LIFE LESSONS

MMM's
MEDITATION, MEDIUMS, METAPHYSICS, MUD, MUSIC, MANIFESTING

NNN's
NAMES, NATURE, NEIGHBORS, NOW

OOO's
ON-PURPOSE, OPENNESS, OPTIMISM

PPP's
PROSPERITY, PROTECTION, PRAYERS, PSYCHOMETRY, PAST LIVES

QQQ's
QUESTION, QUICKLY, QUEST

RRR's
RELATIONSHIPS, RIGHT OR WRONG, RESPECT

SSS's
SELF ESTEEM, SHOULDS, SOULS & SOUL AGREEMENTS, STRESS, SEERS

TTT's
TODAY, THOUGHTS, TRUTH, TELEPATHY

UUU's
UNIVERSAL LAWS OF LOVE

VVV's
VIBRATIONS, VOICES, VISIONS

WWW's
WEATHER, WISDOM, WORK, WISE WOMEN & WIZARDS

Introduction

BREATHE DEEPLY ... CLEAR YOUR MIND OPEN YOUR AWARENESS

Life is truly just an adventure; a journey, a series of lessons. Laugh at yourself at least once each day. Lighten up. When you make what you consider a mistake, congratulate yourself for a lesson well learned! Make that mistake as big as you would any success; big enough to sign your name to! Let the world know that you're succeeding in learning life's lessons, and that you are ready to live to the fullest!

Instinct, intuition or psychic ability; perhaps it's all the same. The exercises and chapters in this book are designed to assist in making Your Life easier, full, more enjoyable, more intuitive, and lighter. The intent is to infuse more kindness, love, and awareness back into our world. Peace is truly a wonderful way to live. Peace can be exciting and joyful, respectful and alive!

If you don't want your life to change, don't read this book!

As a psychic medium, my clients have been asking me for a long time for a different type of self-help, self-empowerment, and light-worker kind of book. Exercises, examples, and understanding have been their criteria. This book was born to help feed that thirst for knowledge and direction. This revised book is about how to be our best, most whole intuitive human beings, and covers the topics I have been asked about the most. The prior missing chapters and exercises are included here, as well as corrections missed in the first publication (if you have a copy of that first publication, I'm sorry about all those mistakes; it was beyond my control). Please enjoy this revision!

On a larger perspective, as our Earth continues to change its course, its geography and its weather, the souls living upon it (that's us) will be best served to be aware of the current and coming environmental and consciousness changes in order to survive easily and well. The joy of this shift is that we are moving into a time of higher consciousness and awareness.

It is not difficult to notice the changes happening to our planet; the acceleration of weather patterns such as volcanoes erupting, earthquakes of great magnitude, floods, hurricanes and tornados, droughts, storms, new islands emerging, land eroding and disappearing ... this will continue. The feelings these changes can evoke in us may seem like chaos; it is important for us all to stay clear, balanced, intuitive and aware during these times. It can be exciting and challenging rather than frightening and threatening if we make the right choices, and stay tuned in to our intuition (it's always there!). The channeled information I have received for the past twenty years has been encouraging that we will not only survive these changes, but excel because of them.

When we decide to take control of our lives, and live with this planet in Light, rather than simply existing and struggling, we can be part of the grand transition that is upon us. So herein lay some ideas for living a full, aware, joyful life so that you might be ready for whatever awaits you.

You may have felt the acceleration of time; that life is almost speeding past, with barely enough time to catch your breath. Well, catching your breath is most important, and you'll read about breathing, balance, and living in this world at its current speed. If you choose to continue, you'll also read about the importance of finding a place where time stands still so that you can center, regroup, find peace and be effective again.

Whether you've been feeling that you're part of something bigger, that something larger than life as we've known it is coming, or that you just feel the need to improve your life and gain a breath of understanding, the ideas in this book may appeal to you and the exercises may be practical enough to help you get wherever you're going.

The chapters are woven together so that you might choose to go from one concept to the next, and then back again to gain greater understanding. Have fun implementing some ideas in your life; notice how people react differently to you when you act differently around them. Decide to make solid choices, be aware of the coming changes, and enjoy this lifetime!

Remember, this is Your Life. Everything you choose to do each day is important, as you have given up a day of your life to do it. Choose wisely, pay attention, live, laugh, and love. Be on purpose.

The transitions occurring upon the Earth bring a need to focus on Soul Awareness, on our part in this world, and the consciousness shift that is occurring. As a Medium and a Channel, I have been told that the timing is now. Find your place and your contribution. In order to do this, knowing yourself, coming to peace with yourself, and loving yourself and the world you live in are essential. The purpose of this book is to achieve these things, by giving you tools and examples to incorporate in your life. Happy reading and joyous living!

AAA's

Affirmations, Attitude, Awareness, Alignment, Angels, Auras

Align yourself as you will.
Alignment with the angels may bring
you greater awareness and a positive attitude.

Affirmations

Affirmations are positive statements we use which can change our thoughts and therefore change our circumstances and the reality we create for ourselves, for the better. You are *affirming* (or saying yes! to) what you do want to create. Affirmations are just for you, they are not for you to say for another. Certainly share what works for you if you so desire, and remember that we're all on our own unique journey. Do create your own incredible life! Pay attention!

When using affirmations, always take a deep, cleansing Breath of Life (unconditional love), feel the smile in your heart make it all the way to your face (a smile is what gives your face value), and gently exhale all the negative stuff that has accumulated. For the moment at least, know that all is well. If you find an affirmation that you'd like to be true for you, but feel that you don't believe it yet; say it anyway! This is how it works: when you finally believe it, you'll see it. Until then you'll simply get more of the same that you've always gotten. If you're good with that, and grateful for what you have, good for you!

While you are practicing your affirmations, you may process through many emotions for a few hours or days until the positive statement begins to stick; continue to repeat it silently and/or aloud. Have faith in your ability to create your life. It will become true for you just as soon as you believe it. Your old thoughts, statements or belief systems may become clear during this process also; just notice and keep shifting into your new, chosen way of living! Let go of all that is not productive for you.

At the end of each chapter in this book, you'll find an affirmation to use if you so choose, related to that topic. Use any or all of these statements. Write them down. Say them aloud as often as possible, and silently at least 100 times a day. Have your favorite positive statement ready to use to immediately replace any negative thought that happens by habit. Watch your world change! Watch as people around you react differently to you as you create a better and more purposeful world for you. As you do this, the effect ripples out and you will be helping to positively affect the world as you know it. Thank you! This is you showing up for your Life, noticing how you want it to be, and taking control of making it so while you do your journey.

All of the affirmations at the end of each chapter remind you to take a breath when affirming; love you as you do so, and be gentle and understanding with yourself as you continue to grow on this journey. Affirmations are always in the now ... the truth as you want it already exists. We just need to look in the correct direction, and we will experience the reality we truly want.

BREATHE AND AFFIRM:

I CHOOSE TO POSITIVELY CREATE MY LIFE!

Attitude

How is your attitude? We all exhibit one at any given time ... is it worth catching? Do you have an optimistic view on life, or do expect everything from others? An attitude is how you look at life, as projected by your thoughts, emotions, words and actions in everyday life.

Who has an *attitude*? Surely every day you notice someone else's attitude, especially when they don't care who sees it ... aggressive, assertive, kind, loving, shocking, whatever it might be. Do you notice your own? Do you take responsibility for your attitude? What attitude do you typically carry around with you and show to the world? Do you wonder why people react toward you the way they do? Are you on purpose about your attitude; toward life, toward others, toward yourself?

A positive and optimistic outlook on life translates into a positive, upbeat attitude, and one we strive to keep. It attracts others of like mind and heart. Conversely, negativity and harsh judgment of self and others becomes a sour attitude; one to get over!

Our Attitude is important every day; whether it is in interaction with close family members, with people we don't know, or in just being. Attitude is the outward expression of what you're feeling inside. If your attitude toward yourself is good, then your attitude toward the outside world will reflect that, and vice versa. Having the correct attitude will also attract nice attitudes back to you, like a boomerang.

Rather than judging others in their attitudes, it would behoove each of us to pay attention to our own, and be responsible for how we act, what we say, and how we treat others. We can better inspire the best in us and in others in this way. What's your story? What does the attitude you typically project say about you? Is it how you want to be known? What imprint are you making on this world with the attitude you currently have?

Have you ever had "an attitude" toward someone, walked away or "blown it off" and then discovered that you suddenly are in another interaction with that same person later in the day or the week? Frustrating or embarrassing as this may be, it gives you the chance to correct the karma you created right away, and to take responsibility for all your thoughts, words and deeds. It also gives you opportunity to check your attitude and notice what you intend to portray, with the chance to make a new beginning with that person and yourself (even if you think you'll never see that person again).

Coincidentally (co-**incident**-ally), you may already have an important mutual acquaintance of this person, or may know a relative of this person. Have you made the energetic impression you want to? Have you opened the door for all the good and grace you want in your life? This is a small world, and everyone turns out to be connected in some way. How you choose to be each moment reflects on who you are. Treat all people as you would like to be treated; practice understanding before reacting.

Remember, no one else caused this attitude of yours! You get to take full credit! Others may have pushed a button or two of yours, but they're *your* buttons! How do you want to be; clear of old stuff, practicing gracefulness, or carrying it around like so much worn out baggage? It takes just a simple decision on your part, and you'll be free and clear, ready to have the best attitude ever.

Here is a simple way to look at life:

Easy Rules of Living

1) Show up

... to Your Life. Be fully present each moment. Wake up and say: "Good morning world! It's me again!" Put a huge smile in your heart. You make choices each day; where you want to be, with whom, doing what you want. When you arrive somewhere, to meet a friend or join a party or attend a meeting, are you there (actually fully present) 100%? Remember that each moment is a moment you won't get back; you've given it to something. This is your life, your moment ... if you are going to be somewhere or do something; SHOW UP! Be there absolutely, or do something else! No excuses! It's your life. This is how to live and love life!

2) *Pay attention*

Breathe! In and out ... and notice what's up with you. Then notice where, what, and when about your circumstance. Notice those around you, and the energies surrounding you. Open all your senses and notice what's going on around you. PAY ATTENTION! Single minded focus has its place for this time. When life is happening, you'll want to notice it. Stop once in a while to pay attention again, particularly if you have experienced inexplicable mood changes ... they may be related to something or someone in your environment. Not that you need to respond to everything around you, just notice and remember that You have shown up for this moment and you know all about this moment by paying attention. You can clear any unwanted emotions or energy. Keep breathing, inhaling and exhaling, and keep paying joyful attention!

3) *Tell the truth*

Tell yourself the truth! When you have situations that are awkward or that you deem will hurt others if you speak up for yourself; take a moment. Remember to show up and pay attention. Take your breath, and tell your truth to yourself (whether you like that truth or not). Notice how much clearer you feel. It is always up to others to feel whatever they feel; consequently, always use tact when you are speaking the truth (or speaking anything at all)! There are many social settings where it is not necessary to tell or say anything; just don't make decisions based on others' uncorrected assumptions. We are each entitled to our own opinion, and our own truth, and it is not to be imposed on others, simply to be stated when appropriate. Don't waste your life living by unspoken assumptions! Be at peace with You, and Tell the Truth! Breathe and let go, especially of the small stuff (and it really is all small stuff).

4) Watch for the big picture; Your Intentions Manifest

The Law of Manifestation says that as we know our truth, we feel it, envision it and believe it before we actually see and experience it. When we do these things, the hows of manifesting whatever it is are taken care of. So we use our positive affirmations, we breathe (with a smile) constantly and deeply. We show up for our lives, pay attention, and watch it all unfold! Set your intention, and don't be attached the interim results, rather be grateful for what appears! On your path, you may find circumstances and responses that you didn't think you were asking for ... these are lessons in your life, karma to clear or even old soul agreements. Navigate them, rather than being attached to a result of getting directly from point A to point B. Life is far more interesting than that! Strengthen your intentions and allow the Universe to assist you in creating the Life you want. Affirm, manifest and let go!

Do set your intentions, and allow others a life of their own ... you're only responsible for you. Notice whether or not you do all four things.

Life really can become easier when we follow these simple rules, especially when you're able to speak the truth about you (first to yourself!), without trying to control someone else's emotions. Certainly we can be tactful when we know an emotion another is likely holding, but withholding truth to spare someone pain is not necessarily the right thing to do, as it also may rob them of the opportunity to express a completely different emotion than you expect. Use TACT and certainly compassion! Let others be in control of what they feel, while you stay in control of your own emotions, if you want to be in control of anything at all! Express kindness as you express truth, and give up the attempt to control others' emotions, hence their lives.

Example of use of the four rules in daily life: Susie and Freddie have been together for four years. Life seems outwardly nearly perfect, although Susie feels she isn't in love with Freddie any more, and acts unfriendly toward him. Susie remains in the relationship, working on simply expressing love. She still feels more sadness and resentment every day because she believes that if she tells Freddie her true feelings (her Truth); *she* will hurt *him*, rather than knowing that he is likely to feel hurt and sad because of this Truth. Susie, in this way, is trying to control Freddie's emotions, whether she consciously intends to or not. It is not healthy, helpful or kind to control others. What if Freddie was feeling the same as Susie, and also did not have the courage to speak his truth or allow Susie her emotions? When one of the two actually speak up, it is also highly possible for the other one to feel relief or even happiness. There may even be such new awareness and trust of each other that a new relationship may spring up for them; at the least, a loving

14

letting go may happen. Perhaps a soul contract has been met, or growth paths have separated.

Indeed, we may know the likely outcome of another's emotions, still we need to gently speak and live our life to the best of our ability. It takes courage, awareness, and the desire to be on purpose to know your truth first for yourself (being honest with yourself) and then to share that truth when it involves others. Tact is still important; when, where and how you speak may be taken into consideration, just don't allow excuses to cost too much time! In the example above, it might be easy for Susie to be in the same relationship two years later, saying the time was never right to speak up. Gather courage, breathe deeply, exhale and know and act at the right time! No blaming, no yelling ... relay only expressions of kindness, compassion and gratitude while speaking truth so that you can be heard. Yelling is only loud noise; it does not convey a message that is heard or respected! Usually, it is followed by an apology, and many hurt feelings; all totally unproductive.

Perhaps if Susie would "allow" Freddie the opportunity to get on with his life, he may meet someone who truly loves him (they both might!). If she cares as one human being for another, she will want that for him (if not, and jealousy settles in, then she needs professional help! Sometimes, getting professional help to learn more about Your Self and how to communicate is a great idea). Good, open communication and your attitude are keys to happiness! Shift Happens! Especially when you give it the space and energy to do so.

An exercise for attitude check: First take some time and notice if you are feeling resentment in *any* area of your life. When you identify the area, notice what you would like to be different. This is telling the Truth to You. Are you genuinely happy? Then, as you remember that you are not here to change or control anyone else, notice what you can do to make your life the way you truly want it. When you give yourself all that you want and need, without harm to others, your life becomes purposeful and it is easier to feel "on top of the world" and be happy. Breathe. Choose to breathe in the happiness you truly want, and exhale all the negative emotions you no longer want to keep. Breathe again and let go. Put a smile on your face and into your heart.

Your attitude shows in how you carry yourself physically. Stand tall and breathe in light; exhale all the worries. Imagine great health, flowing energy and that all is well! The smile will appear (bet you can't help it!). Your attitude really matters; if you choose to have a good, positive attitude, it will attract others to you who also have a good, positive attitude. The flip side is that if you choose a rotten or non-caring attitude, you'll attract that too. Now is the time for you to make a choice, to feel and display the attitude of your choice. You'll feel better about you.

You will experience many emotions; be aware of what attitude you typically present to the world when various emotions linger. If you are worrying, fearful, judgmental or sad, notice that these are emotions that travel through; you don't have to keep them! Joy is our natural state of being. Choose the attitude you want in life, and do your best to always have it! Take time to honor what you feel, let it pass, and get back to happiness!

BREATHE AND AFFIRM:

I HAVE A JOYFUL, POSITIVE ATTITUDE TODAY!

Awareness

What are you aware of? Are you aware of Your Self? Of others?   The World?   Your work?   Material things? Emotional states? Mental chatter? Nothing? Something?

Why is it important to be aware?   This is about the awareness that comes from paying attention on many levels; about a true awareness of Life and all things in it (living or otherwise). Yes, being aware and being centered is of utmost importance! We're talking about being fully present in Your Life. Breathing deeply and releasing. Loving the world as it is; finding simple ways to gracefully contribute to keeping it wonderful or making it better.

Do you realize that **Your Life is up to you**? Hopefully, you're *aware* that you can control the thoughts you have; that your thoughts dictate your words, so you're responsible for them too. And your words dictate your actions (can't blame those on anyone else), your actions define your character (yep, that's you), and your character becomes your Destiny.   So, being aware of your Self and your Thoughts is a beginning to deciding how you want Your Life to be. The big question is "How do I become aware?" It's rather simple, really.

Exercise for awareness: First, become *centered* and *quiet* in yourself. If you meditate (in a simple and passive way), you have probably felt the quietness and centering. Breathing to or from your Center will help you become quiet. The chapter on breathing will give you in depth details on how to do this, and how often to do it.

Next is to *pay attention*. What would you imagine is worth paying attention to? Think about this. Sometimes we find that what we have been paying most attention to doesn't deserve so much of our time and energy. And why is it called "paying" attention anyway? Is it perhaps because it can cost us to focus our attention? What happens when you focus your attention toward something truly important? Is that easier? Does it make other things seem less important? Notice that you get what you pay attention to or focus on. If there is something you want, doesn't it make sense to focus on it?

Now that you're quiet, centered and paying attention, notice what has become important to you. Once your mental chatter has been sufficiently tuned out, your physical body will not be the primary focus at the moment; your emotions will become tempered and you will feel the peace within. Your inner guidance and wisdom will be simply and effortlessly at the fore as your attention is now on your Self / Soul. Your attention will not be on what you're wearing for dinner, but on much larger and more important things. Do this and notice what you pay attention to.

It's important to be aware of Your Self, your needs, your welfare, your emotions, your physical body, and your mental activity. Remember, you are not your body; you are not your mind; you are not your emotions. You are a Soul living *in* your body, complete *with* this mind, and *with* these emotions. You can be in control of you, rather than letting your emotions and thoughts control you, by simply being aware.

Once you take care of you, be aware of your surroundings, including where you live and the planet you live on, the people in your life, and people around you whom you have yet to meet.

Be aware of your Self throughout the day, and pay attention to what you notice; you might become aware of something big that you can have effect on! Continue to breathe in peace and calmness.

BREATHE AND AFFIRM:

I BREATHE IN JOY, AND CHOOSE TO BE AWARE!

Alignment

Now that you have a great Attitude, you've checked all your judgment at the door, and you are in Awareness, let's check out your Alignment.

The tires on your car need to be in alignment (lined up with each other and the car) to take you around easily; if they're not aligned, they will wear unevenly, wearing out eventually, and they won't give you a good ride in the meantime. So it is in Life. If we're not aligned with it, we go down paths we sometimes wish we hadn't, wearing unevenly, wearing ourselves out eventually when we don't *pay attention* and consequently don't stay in alignment, and we don't necessarily get a good ride (and it's all about the journey!). And hopefully we learn anyway we turn ...

Exercise for being in alignment: Go outside (outdoors, wherever there's a tree). Stand next to the tree. Take a deep breath in and then exhale slowly. Reach out one hand and touch the tree. Breathe again. Notice the tree, how it looks, smells, feels. Breathe again with the intent of feeling just like the tree, rooted into the earth, strong, flexible, aware, centered, and free. Notice when you feel *aligned* with the tree. Notice the tree is absolutely free of negative emotions.

You can also do this with another person, or with any living part of nature. Notice when you do this exercise if your perspective changes (on Life, your problems, other people, etc.). The intent with alignment is awareness, peace, perspective and living Life to its fullest. It brings you into alignment with your intuitive flow.

When you are in alignment with Your Self and with your higher guidance, it is easier to be in alignment with All That Is. This means everything and everyone you come in contact with, you will be more easily in alignment with. Your path will be clearer, moment by moment, even if you don't immediately see the end result. It, and we, are all connected.

BREATHE AND AFFIRM:

I AM GRACEFULLY IN ALIGNMENT
WITH THE FLOW OF LIFE.

Angels

Do you know them? Do you feel them around you? Of course they're right there, and they soak up the gratitude you send them. No need to pray for the angels, just say thanks, send gratitude and listen to them.

Angels are around us always. When I was a little girl, I knew the names of two primary angels who were around me always. Trust that they are among us; they love you. Thank them often for being here and it will be easier to notice them. They hear your prayers. Ignore anyone who doubts what you know about the angels. Angels belong to no one. Some will be just around you, though most are with many people at once. I do not call those two angels "mine"; just special.

Exercise for recognizing angels around you: Get in a quiet space, close your eyes and take that nice, cleansing deep breath and exhale. As you begin to feel serene, ask that one or two of the angels around you make themselves known to you. Open your senses so that you may feel, sense, see or hear them.

One at a time is easiest, so that then you may ask each one how you can know them in the future, or what they like to be called. You may find comfort in knowing they're simply there, or each one may let you know that they have a specific purpose to be with you. There may be hundreds of angels around you.

There is no burden too great for an angel, as they simply take our worries and burdens to transmute into Light, while spreading the Light back to us. There is no task too great for them. Earth Angels are living people who seem to always be performing angelic deeds. Simply by existing, they brighten our lives. Do you know any of these? They are gentle souls who have been in the angelic realm in other existences; they usually have had choice to come back to the human experience to help. Show them love and gratitude too! Honor the angels, and they will continue to honor you, whether or not you see or feel them.

BREATHE AND AFFIRM:

**I GRATEFULLY ACKNOWLEDGE
THE ANGELS AROUND ME.**

Auras

The energetic field around each of us, and around all living things, is often called an aura. This energy field is the extension of you that is not densely physical. It can be felt by most people, and seen by some.

You may have noticed when you're in the presence of another person (especially when you're paying attention), that at some point of physical closeness to them, you and they will begin to feel that their "personal space" is being invaded, or that you have really "connected" with them. This is because of the energetic field; when yours meets theirs it is similar, although softer, to actually bumping physical bodies. You will both feel it.

Paying attention to auras of other people will help you to notice that which is most important; it will assist you to know how to proceed with them. Paying attention to your own aura allows you to be at your clearest in any situation.

Exercise for feeling your energy/aura: Sit quietly, and take a deep breath in, and then exhale. Rub your palms together rather vigorously; as you stop, very slowly pull your hands apart. You will be able to feel the strength of the energy you've "stirred up" between your palms. As you continue to move your hands gently away from each other, notice at what point the energy seems to end. This energy is the same as the field around you (which is actually you extending out from your physical body).

As you become more aware of your Self, you may use your breath to expand your aura as large as you'd like, or to tuck it in. You, and therefore your auric field, are pure unconditional love, so as you use your breath in this exercise, imagine the empowerment you may feel as you expand your Self as a loving being.

Some folks see colors in the aura of others. Colors of the chakra are sometimes visible, and so are emotions and illnesses visible as color or vibration. Different areas around the body usually have different colors. Seeing the aura allows one to notice where a person is out of balance or needs healing. Energetic healing, acupuncture, and chakra balancing can help to improve the auric balance of a person, physically, mentally, emotionally and spiritually.

The colors seen may be unique to the seer; whether you are seeing emotions, chakras, dis-ease, healing abilities or something else, you may see someone's aura differently than another does. There is more than one possible energetic experience to be seen. It is possible to feel or notice an aura rather than to visualize it; we still may know about another's energy field without actually "seeing" it. The more tuned in and quiet you become, the easier it is to know about auras.

Remember that you are not a physical body; just in one. Nurture the unconditional love that is you, and notice how well your whole being functions!

BREATHE AND AFFIRM:

**I BREATHE IN LOVE, EXHALE GENTLY,
AND DISCOVER MY OWN BEAUTIFUL AURA.**

BBB's

Breath & Breathing, Balance, Busi-ness, Being

Breathe well; your Life depends on it!
Without Breath, we are a soul without a body.

Breath & Breathing

How important is Breath; *Your* Breath and *Your* Breathing pattern? Do you ever think about your Breath? When and how do you breathe? We're talking about what **Breath** is for (not talking about the smell)! What happens if you don't breathe?

Breath is so natural; it comes as part of the package when we sign up for these bodies, this life! It is an automatic response ... to life itself; think of an infant when just born ... when it takes a first breath, or a person at the end of life who takes their last breath. Perhaps Breath is Life. What does happen if you stop breathing? *When you breathe you inspire. When you don't breathe, you expire.*

To think that breathing is inspiring! It can be, especially when it's intentional. As we grow up, most of us have learned by patterning to breathe in a very shallow way. Notice right now if your inhale is all the way down to your navel (as a baby breathes), or does it stop somewhere in your throat or chest?

Emotion may be stuck where you stop breathing (have you ever "choked" on an emotion?).

There are many benefits to breathing deeply. The first is that taking a deep breath and exhaling slowly all the way is an incredible stress reducer ... especially if you do it again and again. Did you just practice breathing? Felt good didn't it? If you continue to breathe deeply and purposefully often, it will become habit (a good habit).

Breathing well and deeply will help dissipate any negative emotions you may be holding, while reducing stress, if you breathe with that intent. Have you ever been really angry? Remember where your breath was? Was it in your throat? Have you experienced what happens when you're angry and you decide to breathe? Many people refuse to breathe when they're angry; they don't know why at the moment, but it calms them and breaks the anger energy so they can no longer hold it at that level. Try a new motto or mantra for yourself: "BREATHE!" Use it anytime you ... well just anytime at all. If you happen to be around someone else holding their breath, and you are Aware of their discomfort, just *breathe* yourself and they might notice; others often subconsciously breathe deeper right then. Notice the change of energy in the air, and it occurred without effort!

Breathing deeply and regularly will also help you to process other emotions quickly. We all experience a range of emotions through our life; the objective is to not let the negative ones hold us for too long. So we Breathe.

Breathing also helps in oxygenating our bodies; we need oxygen to survive, agreed? When our breathing is shallow, less oxygen is brought into the body. So, with purposeful deep breathing, you can send oxygen to your brain (most of us can use more of that!), to your lungs, and to every part of your body. Thoughts may become clear, health may be improved, stress will begin to leave, intuition becomes clearer, and your cells will function better than ever! Why not *Breathe*?

Can you think of any time that shallow breathing (or not breathing at all) is better than breathing well? If you'd like to be more in control of your life, Breath is the key. You are not your brain; logical thinking and over thinking will only create more stress in time, particularly when unmonitored. Use your brain to program positive, healthy thinking ... it is *You* using your brain, though (You are not your brain!). You also are not your emotions ... same thing applies; train yourself to experience joy as often as possible. You are a soul in a body; the current models come complete with brains and emotions and miraculous automatic functions. With proper breath, we operate as whole human beings (souls in bodies) as highly functioning as possible.

Clients have come to seek my insight and advice on just about everything imaginable; often people will arrive agitated about something in their life. To get beyond what they're feeling (as I feel it too) so that we might get to the true issue, I will ask them to take a breath and let go for a moment. Most often people do, and they feel a bit better right then. Occasionally a person will actually say "I can't now! I have to worry about this and figure it out! Maybe I'll breathe tomorrow!" What will tomorrow bring if we don't breathe enough to get there? When we breathe well enough any real issues will remain, the small stuff will fall away, and we will be able to see more clearly to deal with whatever is on our journey from a higher and calmer perspective.

Breath is key to passive meditation (which is discussed in depth in the chapter "Meditation"). This is a method of being in awareness of you as a Soul; You that is in that body of yours. Take some still time every day and focus on your breath (just breathe!). Notice how calm, clear and happy you become.

Keep breathing!

The best Breath is full of fresh, clean air! High test! Many smokers come to me to stop smoking through hypnotherapy; most are natural meditators and just enjoy the breaks throughout the day to breathe deeply (thinking they need a cigarette to do so) for stress reduction. Most have not been taught how to reduce stress in any other way, nor do they know about the significance of breathing in clean air full of oxygen, and exhaling the built up carbon dioxide and negativity. Even in awareness of the unhealthy chemicals in their cigarette, there seems to be a lack of awareness about the pollution their cigarette is contributing to an already polluted air. The habit is a mental one, not a physical one. Taking breathing breaks is important for everyone to do, and respecting each other's air space (and the quality of it) will add to our quality of life. Practice putting a smile in your heart and releasing stress as you breathe. Your life depends on it!

BREATHE AND AFFIRM:

I BREATHE NOW WITH GRATITUDE AND JOY.

Balance

Do you balance between work and play, sleeping and eating? There are different kinds of balance; here we'll address the balance between the emotional, mental, physical and spiritual aspects (all part but not sides) of You. You are a Whole Being.

What does this mean for you? Are you an athlete, with most of your focus on your physical body? Are you primarily using your mental facilities? Do you emote over every little thing? Or do you pursue spiritual aspects all the time?

The point is that too much focus on any one aspect of you may lead to neglect of the other aspects of you. So, to balance all aspects of One's Self means to pay attention to each of these aspects each day. To not balance is like putting consistent pressure on just one or two legs of a four legged stool, pretty soon the stool is bound to tip over. Are you a human being or a human doing?

Exercise for balance: To begin, notice what aspect your primary focus has been on. Please do not degrade yourself for over focusing on this aspect, instead congratulate yourself for your ability to focus at all! Make some new decisions on how to spend time with the rest of your Self so that from a place of balance you can go back to physical training, mental acuity, emotional release, spiritual focus or that which you intend to be the greatest part of your life. Continual balance is important for success, however, and you may discover that you have several intentions involving all aspects of you, rather than just one.

Now, stop what you're doing for a moment. Take that ever precious deep breath, and exhale. Choose a different aspect of yourself that you have not been focusing on (mental, physical, spiritual, emotional), and decide to focus on that aspect for a few minutes or an hour. Remember during this exercise that this is not a separate part or side of you; you are completely connected as one being, these are simply pieces of the same puzzle that can't be put together until the whole is recognized. By honoring and paying attention to all of you is the way we begin to feel whole, clear, confident, and balanced.

You may get a different perspective when going out for a walk or run after being sequestered in a position of heavy mental activity for a length of time. You might feel renewed, or simply have a brainstorm (which might have been the goal), by changing the focus to another aspect of Self for even a moment. Conversely, if you've been training for a marathon, you may have a much needed rest by doing some type of mental activity while sitting. As simple or mundane as this might sound, most of us may recognize the need for this, and still don't do it. Change that!

Are you aware of the whole you? Can you see how life may be easier if you honor all of you? You may still excel in your chosen field or endeavor.

Balance is also about not biting off more than you can chew. Committing one's self without keeping balance in mind seems to be a malady of today's society. Commitment is excellent when combined with knowing and honoring one's self enough to factor in balance. Only then can we be superb at what we've chosen to be committed to. How often do you make a commitment without thinking and feeling it through for even a full minute? How often do you avoid commitment altogether? If it's the latter, is it perhaps because you haven't gathered how to take on a commitment and stay in balance? It's time to pay attention to what happens when and if you're out of balance.

Example: Guy has discovered carpal tunnel syndrome in his right wrist; he works on his computer 14 to 16 hours a day, and leads an otherwise sedentary lifestyle. He thinks the only option for this dis-ease (discomfort) in his body is surgery so that he can maintain his lifestyle. Perhaps if he spent some time with a different activity, one that engages other aspects of him, such as baseball, tennis, yoga, etc., his wrist may get different stimulation and circulation, and may heal on its own. The rest of him may come into balance, and the pressure off his right wrist could re-balance. Imagine if he had always been in balance; would he have developed this malady in the first place?

Universally, we listen to pain. Often we treat the pain, rather than the cause. When pain comes, it is to remind us to pay attention, look at our life, and get in balance! Live on purpose and in balance so that you don't need that reminder (that Universal two by four that you can't ignore).

Remember that one definition of insanity is doing the same thing over and over again, expecting a different result!

BREATHE AND AFFIRM:

I CHOOSE BALANCE EVERY DAY!

Busi-ness

How busy are you? Is it satisfying? Do you "flit" from one thing to the next, often doing two or three things at once? You have mastered multi-tasking, you say? And do you feel happy and balanced that you have? Or when you do notice, do you feel rushed and unsatisfied? How many breaths have you taken during these times; during your day? Have you stopped to be grateful for each accomplishment? Notice, for you, how much multi-tasking you can do and still feel joy and the correct balance of drive. Do you easily pay attention to your intuition when you are busy? Have you exhausted yourself or energized yourself? Have your priorities become mixed up? Are they your priorities or someone else's? Whew … take a breath! Just notice.

It is easier to receive the fulfillment we're after when we take a few moments to appreciate all that we're able to do, and to be purposeful in what we do. What is the business you're in? Is it the busi-ness of raising children? The busi-ness of real estate, law, department store, or …? The busy*ness* of life easily takes us away from the full*ness* of life and the joy of it. Especially when life is extra full, it is important to stop, enjoy and appreciate it. Fulfillment is a feeling we achieve when we notice energy, relaxation and joy at the end of the day, after work and play. Gratitude and intuition helps balance busy lives, as it gives us time to reflect. Do what you love; others will love you for it, and every day will feel like play rather than busy work.

In this fashion, we re-program ourselves to feel contentment most often, rather than the resentment and stress that busy lives often promote. Contentment and happiness are bi-products of joy, our natural state of being and your birthright. Seek it! Be it! Watch your life transform and time expand.

BREATHE AND AFFIRM:

I CHOOSE A MOMENT OF PEACE
WITH EACH BREATH I TAKE.

Being

Are you a human being or a human doing? Do you find yourself always reacting? When we become still for a moment or two, we can remember who we are and can begin to know our life purpose. A being (like you) is a Soul in a body, any type of body! You are an intuitive being. Once we remember how to breathe, we master being a *being*, then it is easier to more effectively *do* something.

Exercise for truly being: Begin by breathing and desiring to simply be, at least for the moment, and to be the best You possible. What does that mean? Watch, listen, and observe life around you for a moment, without judging or reacting to it. If you've been busy working, running around, raising children, etc., and not paying attention, pretty soon you're likely to run out of breath and steam (if you haven't already). Breathe as you observe in this fashion, and know that you are in this world, not of it. Meditate passively and quietly.

Put a smile in your heart and let it reach your face. All is well; it is as it is. Just be.

By knowing who you are as a Being, decide to honor you, reduce stress, and discover why you're here on this planet in this life with this body, mind and emotions. Once you discover this (future chapters such as "Meditation" will help you find out how!), you may go on about your business, although this time you'll be in the flow of Your Life, unnecessary things will fall away, and you'll begin to attract all that you really want and need.

Do you know that doing nothing is productive? We're not talking about laziness, just the natural instinct to sometimes be still, to visit nature, or to just breathe or meditate. Try it! Let go of guilt and other old useless patterns and emotions you might have kept. Just be, and recharge!

Rules for Being Human

You will receive a body. You may like it or hate it, but it will be yours for as long as you live. How you take care of it or fail to take care of it can make an enormous difference in the quality of your life.

You will learn lessons. You are enrolled in a full-time school called Life. Each day, you will be presented with opportunities to learn what you need to know. The lessons presented are often completely different from those you THINK you need.

There are no mistakes – only lessons. Growth is a process of trial and error and experimentation. You can learn as much from failure as you can from success.

A lesson is repeated until it is learned. A lesson will be presented to you in various forms until you have learned it. When you have learned it (as evidenced by a change in your attitude and behavior), then you can go on to the next lesson.

Learning lessons does not end. There is no stage of life that does not contain some lessons. As long as you live, there will be something more to learn.

"There" is no better than "here". When your "there" has become a "here", you will obtain another "there" that will again look better than your "here". Don't be fooled by believing that the unattainable is better than what you have.

Others are merely mirrors of you. You cannot love or hate something about another person unless it reflects something you love or hate about yourself. When tempted to criticize others, ask yourself why you feel so strongly.

What you make of your life is up to you. You have all the tools and resources you need. Remember that through desire, goal-setting and unflagging effort you can have anything you want. Persistence is the key to success.

The answers lie within you. The solutions to all of life's problems lie within your grasp. All you need to do is ask, listen and trust.

You will forget all this. Unless you consistently stay focused on the goals you have set for yourself, everything you've just read won't mean a thing.

~ Anonymous

Being a soul in a human body and walking in this world as such, is a choice. Making it your intent to enjoy Life in awareness, kindness and with inspiration may just make this an incredible, delightful journey!

BREATHE AND AFFIRM:

I CHOOSE TO BE AND TO BREATHE!

CCC's

Clarity, Clearing & Cleansing, Channeling, Clairs, Crystals

Clear, cleanse, and center yourself so that you may find clarity and truth in all things.

Clarity

How often do you search for clarity? How often do you trudge along in chaos or drama, not thinking as clearly as possible? How much struggle is in your life because you aren't clear about who you are, where you're going, what's happening in your life, or how you're going to get through it all (or all of the above)?

Would you like to have a breather? Would you like to be more purposeful and clear throughout your day and in all your interactions?

Exercise for clarity: Getting clarity is a great priority for you to have! This means getting clear. So first breathe! It truly is the first step to clarity, as it begins to clear away the stress and the fog, particularly when you exhale! This will help you to identify and acknowledge your intuition. So breathe in nice, clear air, with a smile and no thoughts. Let go of absolutely everything!

The next step is meditation, or simply focused breathing with an intent on clearing your mind of chatter, your heart of emotions (just stay in unconditional love and out of judgment), and allow your body and mind simply to relax and be. Take at least fifteen minutes until you've done this many times, at which time you'll "get there" quickly.

Bring into your attention only that which you would like clarity on. Let all the emotions attached to this issue float away. Look at it for what it is, as though you are simply an observer. Do not try to analyze it (your brain is in hibernate mode, remember). *Sense* and *know* whatever wisdom there is to be gained regarding this issue. Do your best not to argue with the clarity that is given to you; have gratitude for it, and imagine carrying on while using your newfound knowledge. Also recognize that peace may come now, and clarity later. Patience!

Breathe again. Allow the energy that used to surround this issue to stay gone; it is no longer useful to you (you can send thanks to it, if you'd like). Notice how easy it is to gain and have clarity. You may also have more energy after this brief exercise. Perhaps you'll focus on clarity more often! It's a wonderful practice to do twice daily!

BREATHE AND AFFIRM:

I GRATEFULLY ACCEPT CLARITY.

Clearing and Cleansing

What does it mean to clear and/or cleanse? Why and when do we need to do it? What would you clear or cleanse anyway?

Do you ever walk into a place (someone's home, a department store, a party, etc.) and suddenly feel different? As though the air is heavier or lighter? Oppressed, freer, confused? Feel as though you wanted to leave a minute ago, or as though you could stay forever? The energies in the space are what you're feeling. They are most likely residues from people who are or were there. It's similar to someone tracking mud through a house, or someone joyously dancing around leaving sparkly light everywhere. Which place would you rather stay in?

We can each be responsible for the energy we carry around and leave behind. Many people are not aware, and the rest are then subjected to what they leave behind. We learn to adapt by knowing ourselves, and clearing and cleansing without judging. When we carry that good attitude, mixed in with kindness and joy, we have an aura that's pleasant and leaves an area clean. If you walk into an area that's heavier, it can be quietly cleared and cleansed by you (without a production!). There are many ways to accomplish this.

Exercise for clearing and cleansing you: First have a strong intent that you wish to be *cleared* of all negative, dark and/or heavy thoughts and emotions, and *cleansed* of all negative, dark and/or heavy energetic things. It doesn't matter whether these were generated by you or others; you need to simply focus on what you want now rather than the past.

Imagine the beautiful white light, stronger than a flashlight beam, beginning from above you or from a tiny place within your heart. Know that this Light is pure unconditional love. As you state your intent, expand that Light throughout your entire physical body, see and feel it stretch out beyond the body as far as your energy goes. As this occurs, allow the Light to take the place of all negativity and recharge you with simple calm love.

You may find success using a plant called sage, bundled and lit, to cleanse areas and/or themselves. This can be done simply and with the same clear intent. Walking in a clockwise or sunwise direction, hold the sage bundle out (lit, just smoldering, and held over a small tray or plate to catch any ashes) and in front of you, thinking and stating your loving, cleansing intent as you move about your home, office or room. The smoke from the sage is intended to clear away the old or negative. Make a loving statement of your intent while doing this. You may also use the sage to cleanse the aura around you and anyone else willingly participating.

As you complete this exercise, you may also protect from any unwanted energies by making such a statement and then imagine sealing this wonderful Light around you ... imagine it sealed with steel, or with reflective mirrors that send all negative energy heading your way out into the Universe to be transmuted into Light. Include joy as you do.

Choose to cleanse, clear and protect (CCP) on a regular basis, perhaps twice a day, with reinforcement as you feel necessary. As this becomes habit, you will notice strength and self-confidence, and that you've begun doing this subconsciously.

Good for you! It's easier now for you to know how *you* are feeling, amidst the clamor of the rest of the world, and to clear the "stuff" from you while remaining empathetic with others. Move easily and joyously again!

Reinforce CCP as often as you choose throughout your day or week. If you are extremely sensitive, and find this is not a strong enough exercise for you, I recommend that you have true, in depth intuitive training to develop additional strong methods for maintaining a clear environment. You will notice easier breathing with the natural flow of life when you clear and cleanse regularly.

After cleansing, clearing and protecting, it becomes easier and easier to meditate clearly. Be clear and joyful!

BREATHE AND AFFIRM:

**I JOYFULLY AND FULLY BREATHE
(IN AND OUT)
AND CLEAR MY BEING.**

Channeling

Channeling is a word with many meanings. As a Medium, deceased loved ones appear to me and give messages via me to their loved ones still here on Earth; actual channeling is a different experience than that or than communicating with guides or angels. Channeling happens when an entity, guide, or group of entities are allowed to communicate directly through your physical body (by agreement) either fully or partially. Sometimes this comes through as a strong urge to speak or even a tickle in your throat, inexplicably, and when you don't have a clue as to what is about to come out of your lips! If you choose to channel, or this gift has chosen you, it's always a good idea to have someone with you to take notes so that you can stay in proper awareness of the channel, and be well protected.

I intentionally choose to step away from my body for this channeling, as I know and trust the Source, and can still hear, know and feel all that is being communicated through me while not getting in the way. It is much easier to allow this communication without being in the way of it (as in monitoring how the words come out). The most common channel I do is of the "Council of Light"; a council of the highest order, thirteen Light Beings who have been giving information through me for the past 25+ years. The majority of their information has related to the Transition; the shifting of our world as we know it. It has been about Earth movements and changes, and has evolved additionally into the consciousness shift we have begun. This shift is into a higher vibration, a kinder, more compassionate and aware society of souls.

If you feel you are a channel, it's good to have one-on-one training since this is a highly sensitive state. This training includes daily passive meditative practice, as well as a good grasp of the Universal Laws of Love.

BREATHE AND AFFIRM:

**I ACCEPT THE CLARITY AND THE PURITY
OF THIS WISDOM AS IT FLOWS THROUGH ME.**

Clairs

Let me introduce you to the Clairs! You've probably heard of people who are Clairvoyant; it means those who are *clear seeing*, or who see with their intuitive sight. We often use this as a general description for people who are "psychic". People (you included) receive information about others and about life in many different ways, beyond the five physical senses of sight, sound, smell, taste and feeling.

Often, the reception for an individual comes strongly in one or two ways that are beyond the physical. Sometimes, a person will receive information in many ways. These methods of reception that are beyond the physical are in the realm of psychic, intuitive or metaphysical (beyond the physical).

When you (or anyone) has a vision, or "sees" in their mind's eye rather than seeing with their physical eyes, it is called being clairvoyant. This seeing is not always as clear as, or the same as it is with the physical eyes, although it can be honed to even greater clarity by awareness, practice, and paying attention. The clairvoyant may see a future event or a present circumstance. If you are clairvoyant, a little or a lot, and would like to develop this talent, begin by practicing the stillness we spoke of earlier.

Since these are *senses* *beyond* the five physical ones we most usually focus on, paying attention only to those five senses won't help much in developing one of your "sixth senses". So focus on your Soul a bit every day, stretch *You*, and then your attention to what and how you receive will become easier.

Perhaps you actually hear a voice, in your head or over your shoulder? You're probably clairaudient, or clear hearing. This is not as common for most people, though it does happen and can be improved in the same fashion we just spoke of.

Have you suddenly smelled something that is totally out of context for where you are (the smell of roses perhaps), or have a taste in your mouth out of the blue? These are two more Clairs (Clair means clear), or other ways to be clear ... clear smelling and clear tasting. These Clairs, particularly clear tasting (such as that of tobacco or someone's favorite pie), are less common to experience, yet bring information that quite often clue us in to the presence of a deceased soul, or the opportunity to receive further communications in other fashions. If this happens to you, you may be a medium; pursue it.

Do you feel on an intuitive level; then you may be clairsentient, or clear feeling. This is a more common trait. This "title" recognizes a type of feeling that is different from being empathic (where we actually feel what another is feeling and that emotion is indistinguishable from our own). Clairsentience means that you may know or sense what another person is feeling; you may feel it less strongly but are just as aware of what you feel. We also use this description for those who simply sense things; you may be extra sensitive to your environment and/or other people to the extent you sense beyond the physical.

Clairvoyance has become a catch all term for people who are psychic or intuitive in any manner; and the technicality of the descriptive terms are of lesser importance than actually determining how you receive, and honoring and developing that.

There are more descriptions of the way we intuit our world in other chapters in this book, such as the ones on Empaths, Mediums, Channels, IJK and Psychometrists. Titles or descriptions need not be relied heavily upon; though they are helpful for you to identify how you receive information ... beyond that, it becomes easier to notice and just receive.

Science has told us that most folks only use 10% of their brains. The studies in ESP and metaphysics show that we use the other 90% for intuition of one sort or another. Balanced training and exercise of all our abilities will change how we live on this planet. Just as some people are stronger runners than others and enjoy it more, some people are stronger intuitives (of one sort or another) and may or may not enjoy it more, though typically get much more out of life when they understand and embrace it!

BREATHE AND AFFIRM:

I GRATEFULLY ACCEPT AND TRUST ALL OF WHO I AM.

Crystals

Crystals are energetic rocks produced from the Earth. They may be quite colorful, or very clear, and sometimes both. Often, when we pick up a crystal, you can feel its temperature ... it may be cool or warm. This is one property that crystals have.

When you get very quiet, clear and centered, it is possible to feel other properties of a crystal while holding it in your hand. You may feel a vibration, or a sensation in a particular part of your body, or you may even have a subtle emotional response.

Crystals have been used for healing for eons. If you really pay attention, you realize that crystals have a variety of properties from emotional balancing to physical healing and assisting with connecting beyond this plane of existence.

Exercise for noticing crystal properties: Find a small crystal that you like or are attracted to in some way. Take a calm, deep, cleansing breath and get centered.

Then close your eyes, holding the chosen crystal in the palm of your hand (one at a time, please). Allow your senses to open and notice any sensations at all ... emotional, physical, or spiritual. If you for any reason tend to dismiss what you're receiving, choose for this moment to imagine the truth in your crystals' message.

You will have chosen a crystal that is helpful to you in some way; and that way has just been revealed to you. Smile and breathe in again, this time breathing in all the properties of the crystal, and allowing those to balance or heal you. Allow it to do all the work, gently accepting and trusting. Be grateful.

BREATHE AND AFFIRM:

I LOVINGLY ACCEPT ALL THAT THE CRYSTALS GIVE TO ME!

DDD's

Dimensions, Death, Dreams

*Decide how you're going to Live this Life;
Dying will come soon enough. Live it well!*

Dimensions

There are many descriptions and understandings of dimensions. In the waking world which we walk through, we have created time and space in order to have this physical experience and interaction with each other. As we visit "the worlds beyond", such as where those souls who have crossed over are, those who are stuck in between, as well as angels, guides and other entities are; we experience other dimensions.

You may hear that there are three or four dimensions, or that there are 14 of which we are just discovering. As you continue this journey, you may have heard that there are 112 or 237 different dimensions. These are theories you might want to explore, and there are actually as many or few you can conceive, and as diverse as you can possibly imagine; some even beyond Life as we imagine it. As Souls in this current dimension, we quite simply inhabit a physical body of a particular type, with a brain holding certain types of thoughts, and with emotions of all sorts. Imagine what, and how much more we might be void of the body, mind and emotions.

There is no right or wrong, especially when it comes to dimensions. Whatever you choose to believe, is. The importance of dimensions in this writing is to reinforce that we can be aware of energy and existence beyond our most visible dimensions, and to live wholly and fully we simply pay attention, know that anything is possible, and don't discount that which is not seen with the physical eye.

Living in and understanding the dimension we live in now, may be enough! You might decide to believe that everything is a miracle or nothing is. It's all miraculous!

BREATHE AND AFFIRM:

I SEE ALL OF LIFE AS
A MIRACULOUS POSSIBILITY.

Death

Death is simply a transition from this form of life, from and out of this physical body, to another existence. This I have been shown by those who have "crossed over" (died and still exist) and that I have re-experienced in my death experiences this lifetime.

If you've been reading and paying attention, you'll remember that breath is an energy that may resemble the freedom of our soul in its natural state. Take that a step further and imagine where breath goes when you're not breathing it in, or when you exhale. This living energy (perhaps it's You) exists (hence the word "live"), and is part of All That Is. Using your imagination, and your ability to be still and quiet, ponder the possibilities of life beyond this one ... not just beyond this planet, also beyond these bodies.

The deceased who come with you to speak to you via me, are in this phenomenally blissful place; this state of being.

They show themselves to me in a way that can be described to you for your recognition. It may be their prior physical description as well as their personality as you knew them. Remember that now they have full understanding of the way things are and were; they no longer live in a physical body nor are they burdened with human emotions, although they know and understand them as well. They have no judgment, simply unbiased understanding. They are not looking for apologies, retribution or forgiveness, nor do they want you to suffer because they have left this Earth. They are profoundly joyful and wish you also to be so in this life.

This theme is common for the deceased; for children, for adults, even those who have taken their own lives. Those who have committed suicide go to the same wonderful place as those who have died a "natural" death, who have been taken by disease, and those whose lives have been taken by others. They all look at the life we experience here on Earth as a training ground; no grudges are held! We ultimately all go in one manner or another ...

There are occasionally those whose spirit remains "stuck" in between for a while, who are either not aware of or are in denial of their passing. We assist them to let go, and they too arrive at that beautiful place of peace.

The life review each soul experiences after crossing over seems to vary in length and topics for each soul, as it applies to the life just left. When understanding and non-judgment are realized by the soul, the soul may then go on to another "level". This process may take just moments or perhaps days according to our view of time. Then, from this place of wisdom, the soul of your deceased loved one will contact you.

They always hear when you speak to them. They know you love and miss them, and are most joyous when you are joyous. There is absolutely nothing to be afraid of. They *are* the love that never dies.

When you are the calmest, quietest, least judgmental, and sit with a smile in your heart, you will be able to notice them most easily. Just listen, say hello, and send your Love.

BREATHE AND AFFIRM:

I FULLY BREATHE IN THE BREATH OF LIFE NOW, AND I EXHALE AS I ACCEPT THE LOVING TRANSITION OF OTHERS.

Dreams

We all dream at one time or another, whether we realize it or not, and sometimes more often than other times.   Our dreams may be the time our subconscious gets to work out all the stuff that has gone on in our lives that day or week, or sometimes our dreams may be prophetic. You might even have visions in your sleep, and call them dreams.

Prophetic dreams are dreams of future events. You will see them come to fruition. Often, people are shown future events so that a warning may be issued; other times prophetic dreams come to folks who are simply psychic and either don't pay attention to other intuitive signs or information during the day, or simply have this as their way of receiving.

Vision dreams are more often metaphoric, or have greater impact on coming opportunities for the dreamer or someone in close contact with them. These will seem more like a vision than a dream (more realistic), and are also to be paid attention to.

Write down your vision dreams, and any dreams you remember, as soon as you wake. You might prefer a small recorder to talk into; either way a recording is important. Talk to someone else about what has come to you, and get their input. You'll remember more as you recall your dream out loud.

As in other forms of psychic reception, it will be especially helpful to get in-depth training if you receive in this manner. Quite often, prophetic dreams are very clear, and may be unsettling or disturbing. If this is so, receiving the training to clarify and minimize the potential trauma of these insights can make your life easier, and will give you direction for dispersing this information.

You might give yourself a suggestion just before going to sleep that you'll wake up rested, refreshed and remembering. It really helps!

BREATHE AND AFFIRM:

I REST, DREAM AND REMEMBER WELL.

EEE's

Empaths, Energy, Experience

*Experience the energy of all things and all people;
from this comes empathy and
the ability to understand.*

Empaths

One form of intuition is being empathic. It is actually feeling and experiencing what someone else is feeling or experiencing, as though it is your own experience. This is different than simply knowing or sensing what someone else is feeling.

Being empathic can be difficult and draining, particularly if you don't know that you are empathic. If you don't recognize and honor this ability, and then act on letting the emotions go, you will most likely become like a sponge that has been left in a bowl of water; not knowing what emotions are yours to begin with, and what emotions you are feeling that came from others.

If you are an Empath, I strongly recommend you reread the chapter on clearing and cleansing, and practice the exercises there. Then decide what to do with this gift. If you are a practicing psychic intuitive, speak what you know and feel to whom you're feeling, (*as is appropriate*), then quiet yourself and ask to also receive the advice that is intended for that person.

If you are not a practicing psychic intuitive, and you suddenly feel the inexplicable change within yourself, stop a moment to notice and become aware of your new surroundings. Take a breath, clear, cleanse and protect yourself. This is a delightful rather than fearful thing to do. Pay attention to your "mood swings"; notice if they're yours (if you can relate them to an event or thought, for instance) or not. Either way, ask to let go and release these emotions to the Universe, and to re-experience joy. Have no judgment, and it is not necessary to speak up about it ... just decide whether you want to stay in that current situation or not. Maintain your chosen happy attitude and state of being.

Exercise for Empaths: Practice letting go, clearing and cleansing often. It doesn't do you or anyone else any good to hold on to these emotions that come from someone else. You will still know about that emotion and the person experiencing it, you just won't need to keep it! So sit quietly, intend and ask for higher assistance in being completely rid of the emotions that aren't yours, and remember how you feel when you're content (it's good to have a baseline to return to, such as that you achieve when you've been meditating). Let go and be.

A person can be empathic as well as having other forms of intuitive abilities. People who are Empaths are not being punished! We are in the Universal flow, and have been given this gift (or agreed to come into this Life with it) as a means to understand and help others. Empaths usually learn non-judgment quickly, as we are always also given understanding and compassion with each instance of knowing. As an Empath, this form of intuition is the most difficult to ignore, and one of the most important to respond to. Be grateful to be in such a connected flow of life!

BREATHE AND AFFIRM:

**AS I GRATEFULLY AND DEEPLY INHALE
A CLEANSING BREATHE, I LOVINGLY
EXHALE AND RELEASE ALL.**

Energy

Everything we know is energy. Think about your breath; it's simply energy, isn't it? You may notice the lightness of the energy of your breath, and compare that to the feel of energy of other things. If you consider this breath to be You (Self, Soul, Spirit), then You recognize that we each are simply energy; the energy of unconditional love and part of All That Is. Physical, tangible things are energy in form. It is even possible to energetically change the form of physical items.

Emotions are energy. Pay attention for a moment to the energy of laughter; it can be light. Now pay attention to the energy of anger; it can be quite heavy. How about pure joy? Which types of energy do you prefer? It is a choice that you can make; choose which emotions and energy you want to pay attention to, to hold and to experience. Focusing on unconditional love, bliss and joy and experiencing the lightness of life makes it easier to be a human being with various emotional experiences flowing through.

As human beings we have a full range of emotions; we are of joy, and you do not have to hold any negative emotion at all! What good does it do you to wallow or worry? (The answer is none!) Negative energy, particularly that of heavy negative emotions, often creates dis-ease in the physical body as it can literally change the shapes of the cells. Positive emotions, those kind and loving ones, will promote health, happiness and well-being. It truly is what we do with our emotions that matter.

Thoughts are also energy, and therefore creative as well. Choose them carefully! Thought are things. What you think can and will manifest into being. Long term patterns of thinking a particular way will, whether it's worrying or whether it's optimistic, most certainly bring to your life what you've been thinking (more of the same). Change your thoughts to positive, light energy, and watch your body heal! The energy of thought is the same manifest energy of the physical.

Choose to focus on the most pleasant energies and you will attract more of the same to you. Notice as you breathe naturally and deeply how easy it is to feel the energies around you, and to be in the Flow of Life.

This same unconditional love energy that we are, that flows through our bodies, is also healing. As you stay in the Flow, you might discover that you are a natural healer. You may notice warmth or tingling in your hands from time to time, particularly if you're near someone who is dis-eased or needs physical and emotional healing. Pay attention, and you'll know what to do instinctively (intuitively), or ask for guidance from another healer. If you recognize this in yourself, still honor the privacy and boundaries of others!

Children may be nurtured and taught about thoughts and energy, so that as they grow, their intentions, thoughts and actions are on the correct path. Help them to develop into their best selves!

BREATHE AND AFFIRM:

I LOVINGLY ACKNOWLEDGE THE ENERGY AND LIFE OF ALL THINGS.

Experience

There's an old saying that bad judgment leads to experience, and experience leads to good judgment. Laugh at yourself often for doing this journey well!

Experiencing many aspects of life is important to learn what we're here to learn. Perhaps there really are no mistakes, just lessons. How will we truly grow and learn the lessons that are for each of us, if we don't experience them? Much can be learned from reading, but there's no replacement for actual living.

One of the most often repeated themes in people's journeys is divorce with a feeling of failure (only occasionally of relief and joy). Rather than learning from the relationship experience, understanding Self better, gaining the wisdom and grace to do things differently in the future, and be grateful for the experience, people will allow their grief to become the self-pity that comes with prolonged failure. It takes courage to notice when a relationship is no longer loving and both parties are not moving forward together anymore; and even more courage to bless the other and either deliberately and lovingly work together to change the relationship, or to go on to the next chapter in life, while wishing love for the other person.

Learn from all your relationship experiences, whether they're casual or intense experiences! Otherwise, you'll continue to receive similar types of relationships and encounters until you do; they are the primary source for our growth and ultimate recognition of what Self Love is and how to show others how to love and treat us. Remember that we choose to enter into relationships of all kinds, daily. We are each responsible for our behavior, thoughts and emotions at all times. You may have allowed yourself to stay in a relationship longer than you wished or than is healthy; you are responsible for that action, and for self-forgiveness. Please stay away from blame; take responsibility for your part, as you can only change, correct or improve you!

Take a breath and observe your relationships from a place of non-judgment, awareness and openness to experiencing them from another's' point of view. Make a decision to embrace every experience you have, no matter how pleasant or unpleasant it is. It is easier this way to love your life, learn from it, and be happy. Share your experiences; you are unique and special!

Choosing not to love rather than risking hurt again is a very sad, self-imposed, life sentence! Why live a life of misery? Grieve, and then carry on! Taking time to know and love your Self before entering into a marriage or other close relationship is always a good idea, and can be very enjoyable. Only when you love and like You, can you expect others to. We learn to do this not only from our interactions with others; more often when we have the wonderful opportunity to live with just ourselves for a while. Just You; embrace and enjoy it! Know what it is others will be blessed with when they befriend you.

BREATHE AND AFFIRM:

I AM GRATEFUL FOR ALL MY EXPERIENCES, AND AGREE TO LEARN FROM THEM QUICKLY!

FFF's

Fun, Fear,
Family (and other strange entities),
Forgiveness, Free Will

Exercise your own free will for the good of you,
for it is your will and your thought
that create your Life.

Fun

Fun is essential! Just like sleep. Have lots of fun often! Why would you even think of depriving yourself of fun, or that it isn't as important as sleeping, eating or working? It is releasing, regenerating and can be invigorating.

Fun is part of the essential balance of life. It nurtures perspective, releases stress, facilitates easier breathing and better health, and allows for less judgment of others.

Having fun loosens the knot of over-responsibility. Maintaining respect for others while having fun takes a load off too! Respect others' boundaries, set our own, open your eyes and put a smile in your heart.

Fun keeps us youthful. And do remember that having fun doesn't make you childish; childlike wonder is one thing, acting childishly is another. Have fun! It may be as simple as adding a smile or a dance to what you're already doing; if you choose to do it, you might as well enjoy it! Impulsive fun is the best; schedule it in if you need to though. Get in the habit of having fun; imagine sleeping, eating, playing, working, loving all that you do; it may all be part of your day as you imagine and create it.

If you have difficulty having or finding fun, find a friend who's good at it, and ask them to help you along. If you're good at having fun, you most likely bring others with you; if not, please find a friend who seems to need a bit of encouraging and show them the way (respecting boundaries, of course)! Being a fun loving person may just be our natural state ... let's get it back!

When fun is flowing, so is the Life Flow. Be in it, and you'll notice that it becomes even easier to sense and recognize your intuition.

BREATHE AND AFFIRM:

**I CHOOSE FUN,
AND I RESPECT OTHERS' CHOICES.**

Fear

<u>F</u>alse <u>E</u>vidence <u>A</u>ppearing <u>R</u>eal ... or

<u>F</u>ace the <u>E</u>xit <u>A</u>nd <u>R</u>un!

These are acronyms for fear (F.E.A.R.). It is difficult to hold the energy of love when you focus on fear. The only thing fear is good for is to warn of impending danger (primal fear), otherwise, let it go!

Perhaps this life was meant for you to live it! How much time does it take you to procrastinate due to fear? Imagine the cost ... was there a time when you've allowed fear to control your decisions or paralyze you, and then you finally took action weeks, months or even years later? What if you always acted out of Love rather than fear; listening to your intuition and trusting first? What would you get done sooner, and how much more fun would you have? How quickly would you get your life lessons?

As a society, we fear an awful lot of things; most needlessly ... wasting our own time, energy and life, while creating exactly what we do not want. People often have a debilitating fear of themselves or what they may do or think or may have done or thought. All that any of us have done in this lifetime is an opportunity for joy or an opportunity to learn from.

If you're in elementary school, and you're learning a topic, and you don't get it right the first time, is it appropriate for both the teacher and you to be angry at you? Of course not! It is appropriate for the teacher to find another way to teach you until you get it (imagine how compassionate and loving that is!). Just as in the School of Life that we are all in, learning can be easier when we realize it's just school; don't be afraid of it, rather Show Up for it; Pay Attention to it; Tell the Truth as you know it; and Don't be Attached to the Results!

Set your intentions clearly, however. If what you've learned isn't quite all of it, you'll know pretty quickly, and can continue on your path of learning. The more joyously you do this, the more you embrace life as an opportunity rather than an obligation, the easier it is to learn what you're here to learn, and for those in interaction with you to get what they're here to get with you in their lives. Look for your "Aha" moments with pleasure!

Many times, the fear we experience is of the unknown. For instance, you may be in a relationship or job that hasn't been appropriate for either of you for a very long time, yet you stay because it's familiar. If you're working on the joy of it, and improving your interaction, great! If you're stuck by simple fear of moving on; look at that a moment, and notice if it is so.

So many times a victim will stay with an abuser just because they can no longer see beyond the fear; they know that life can be "really bad", yet it's currently a "bad" situation that is familiar. The same could be true with your work; sometimes a person only knows what they've been doing and for whom, and if all they do is gripe because they are so unhappy there, they've most likely given in to the fear of change. So fear rules their lives.

What we focus on is what we get. Hope is lost when fear is in control. Grab hope, and choose love and loving situations all the time!

Ask yourself if you are allowing fear or love to control your life. Notice. Which do you want to live your life by? There are no ifs, ands or buts here! Choose one way or the other to live by please! Love is the obvious choice, and sometimes that takes courage; think about that a moment - it takes more courage to choose love than to choose fear! How did that happen? It's not rational.

Once you've chosen the most loving path for You, you'll discover it's so much easier and rewarding! That's how you know when you're on the correct path.

BREATHE AND AFFIRM:

TODAY I CHOOSE LOVE!

Family
(*and other strange entities*)

We can learn a lot from our family ... especially from our biological family, although also from our Soul family. Hopefully, we learn to receive and give unconditional love within either unit.

Family tends to stick around, no matter how "dysfunctional" they seem to be. We chose them, just as they chose us, to take this journey together. Occasionally, a family member "gives up" because it's "just too hard" ... this is most often a temporary situation; we go back or they come back, and try again. If you're fortunate, they or you will reconnect and say "I'd like to work on our relationship". When this happens, give it your best, and your kindest self! This is not an opportunity to "air all", rather an opportunity to show up as how you are now and to notice and respect how they are NOW.

I've heard many a client exclaim to me that they can't imagine they're truly related to their family! You may feel the same, or that you are blessed with the most loving or understanding family. Either way, we can learn; anything is possible!

It will be truly wonderful when we can each express gratitude to family members (or others) for "putting us through" such grief, trauma, confusion, etc., because we finally learned from the experiences. Place no blame! Pay attention to your role, and whether or not you are pleased with *your* responses and actions as you interact with these strange entities called siblings, parents or children. It is not for you to change anyone! Let them be who they are, and interact in the highest manner you can muster. If anger abounds, walk away. Come back later when you each agree to act as adults using your best indoor voices.

When we're talking about you being in interaction with children, yours or others, we don't change them either; we notice who they are, and guide them in their direction, by our own marvelous behavior and by loving communication and praise. Isn't that how you'd like to be treated? This doesn't mean the children make all decisions for you, themselves or the household, though ... help them learn to assimilate their needs with the needs of the family or group.

If you're seeking understanding as to why you might have chosen a particular family member in your life, it's helpful to do a Past or Future Life Regression to remember other lifetimes you've shared with this person. Chances are you've created the same theme, and this perspective may assist you in getting the message this lifetime, and then to be able to move forward correctly, differently, and hopefully quickly. In this process, you may also gain insight by doing a Soul Journey during hypnosis.

You did not create this family environment for punishment! Nor did you enter it simply to be honored as being "right". Every person is perfectly different, thank goodness! Find the love within your family unit, and learn from your differences. If you are on a faster spiritual growth path than your family members (or vice versa), so be it. The Soul Family (usually non-blood relatives) that you collect will most likely be at your pace. Love and Learn!

Be grateful for everyone on your path, and for yourself. It is possible to outgrow others; this does not mean you're better or lesser than they are, it just means you're paying attention and getting it! Hooray for you! We'll hope they get it also, in part by being in interaction with you. Be the best sibling, child, parent and friend you can imagine. Be the best to you.

BREATHE AND AFFIRM:

I LOVE MY FAMILY, LEARN FROM THEM, AND I CHOOSE TO BE THE BEST (*family member*) POSSIBLE!

86

Forgiveness

We come into this life to remember Self Love, amongst other things. Each of us, as souls, are like a drop of rain that returns to the ocean (the field of pure potentiality or unconditional love) when we pass away from this lifetime. We have this time and space experience and choose these physical bodies to inhabit to interact with each other, and yet we are never separate from that ocean, that vibration of unconditional love.

Through strife and struggle, through joy and grief, we grow. If this life was void of chaos, what would we learn? We each do our best, and our best to help each other through the tough times. Hopefully, we do our best not to intentionally create difficult times for others. Imagine that without the dark, we might not appreciate the light; it doesn't mean, however, that we need to stay in darkness for any length of time.

Imagine what *your* life journey is about. Is it about remembering Self Love and the fact we're all connected? Is it about remembering that love and abundance are of the same vibration? Is it about remembering that you are an important, unique and magnificent being? It is all this, and more.

This life is like school; you will find that you have teachers in many of the people you encounter throughout your life. Learn from them! In elementary school, if you think, act or speak in an incorrect way, do you need to be punished or lovingly taught the correct way? The latter loving choice, always, of course. Why would you punish yourself when you don't like your thoughts or behavior? You simply notice, and change both. (And perhaps apologize ...).

Be gentle with you, correct those thoughts or behavior, decide you'd like to learn from the experience you've created (especially if someone else has come into interaction with you to inspire your thoughts and actions!), and FORGIVE YOURSELF! There is no need to forgive anyone else; they acted as a guide or teacher for you.

Exercise for forgiveness: It's as simple as saying aloud, to just you: "I forgive me". Take a deep breath, exhale, and say it again. You may have a particular incident in mind as you do this, or you may just want to say it for general purposes; most of us carry guilt around for much of Life, others because it was taught. Correct whatever it is you are feeling guilty about, forgive yourself, and then Let It Go!

We don't need to condone or judge angry or violent behavior; simply learn from it, and assess whether or not it's appropriate in your environment, and move on, all the while surrounding yourself in love. If we don't learn from a person or an event, we'll continue to receive similar people and events (guides and teachers) until we do. Show up and pay attention! Learn! Then forgive you for allowing the same circumstances over and over, and create new and different ones.

This is your life. Live it the absolute best you can. Learn along your journey; laugh, let go, and remember Unconditional Love. The only true forgiveness is that of Your Self.

BREATHE AND AFFIRM:

I FORGIVE ME!

Free Will

Clients often ask me about free will and choice, and about destiny. People who really love life seem to exercise their free will and make great choices, while many people would like to think everything is predetermined so that they have no responsibility for their life or the decisions they make. And then there is fate ...

We do have free will and can make choices, thank goodness. We have the ability to create this life to be any way we would like it to be.

There are some moments in this life that are predetermined, meaning that a particular outcome will happen within a small time frame, although this is more the exception rather than the rule.

Example of free will and choice: Harry decided one night to cut through a dark alley to go to a small neighborhood grocery store. On his way, he was accosted and robbed. As horrible as the experience was, Harry did not change any of his circumstances and continued to complain about the young man who attacked him. There were neighborhoods nearby which had roads that were better lit and where loving people live and watch out for each other. The housing was just as affordable. Harry did not have much self-esteem, and always expected the worst in others. Harry *chose* to live where he lived, to walk where he walked, and to expect what he expected; therefore he got the life he was creating by his thoughts, his free will and his choice. No one else made him think, choose or act in this way.

By noticing our life, we can use our free will and choice to change anything at all about our life; where we live, who we associate with, what we do, how we believe, how we think, how successful we are, and so on. Seek happiness! It's your choice.

Yes, occasionally we will each come across a circumstance that seemingly cannot be avoided. This may well be a predestined moment that we agreed to prior to this life, and something to learn from. Forgive yourself, and move on.

Example of destiny: A young mother was talking with a friend while holding her six year old daughters' hand, all of them standing in her yard in a quiet neighborhood. Suddenly, the little girl abruptly pulled away from her mother to run into the street just as a large truck was speeding down that street. The girl was hit by the truck and was instantly dead. The prior two days, the mother had "saved" her daughter twice from narrow misses with death. This was a case of predetermined outcome, or destiny.

It is not always destiny, although when circumstances repeat, it typically is. And when it is, please remember that it was agreed to by the soul(s) involved, prior to this life. The little soul was in agreement, whether she remembered that in this life or not. She is a happy soul, and her mother has joined her now.

Always, we have the marvelous opportunity of choice; our will is free to choose any path, any journey. We will still create the opportunity to learn all that we have come here to learn, and to enjoy the journey as much as possible. We are best served when we make choices in our own highest and best interest, with conscious intent, wishing success for others as we go forward on our path.

Making yourself look or seem smaller so that someone else may feel better about themselves does not benefit anyone; nor does it work the other way around, so don't buy into it! Every person on this planet has free will and choice; encourage the choices for yourself and others that truly empower you and them. Use your free will to see the best in people, to be the highest example you can, to associate with folks who are excited about being on their particular journey (who are on purpose, showing up, paying attention and telling their truth), and to find the most joyful and supportive place to live (even if you live many places this lifetime!). When you're in touch with your intuition, and breathing well, it's easiest to make great choices for your own life.

Exercise for using free will: You do it every day, whether you consciously realize you're doing it or not! Notice something that hasn't felt right today or yesterday, but that you engage in on a regular basis. Is there anything? Pay attention and ask yourself why you continue to do this. Use your intuition to help you by taking a deep breath and exhaling, imagine not doing this thing or doing it in a different fashion; how does that feel intuitively? Look at all the circumstances surrounding this one thing, and make a new decision, a new choice about how to do it differently or not at all.

If by chance you have said that your boss "makes you" or someone else dictates it, then take the exercise a step farther and remember that it is your choice also to work for that person or to be in interaction with a particular person. If it's part of an agreement you made, do it gratefully or decide to change your life. You do not have to keep the same circumstances! While you do, take responsibility for all your choices, and do them well.

You always have free will and choices to make; when you exercise them for your highest and best good, with no harm to others, everyone wins and you will feel empowered. Take note of that which is beyond your control, and don't waste time trying to change those things; only that which is within your realm and relates to your life. Take responsibility for your whole life. Laugh at you as you've gone through this school of life and all the successes you've had (especially those that may have felt like failures to you at first) as you learn and grow, and celebrate the magnificent being you are on this incredible journey!

You can create a magnificent life for you, so start today!

BREATHE AND AFFIRM:

**I TAKE RESPONSIBILITY FOR MY LIFE
AND MY CHOICES,
AND I CREATE MY BEST LIFE!**

GGG's

*Giving, Gratitude, Guides, Guilt,
Goddess / God / Great Spirit*

*Gratitude creates a heartset that
attracts all that you most love.*

Giving

The joy of giving! Did you know that giving and receiving are essential parts of the same circle? When you give, there must be a willing recipient. When you receive, there must be a willing giver. One does not exist without the other.

Have you ever gone to lengths to gather the perfect birthday present for a dear friend, and then had the friend refuse to accept your gift? How did/would you feel? Perhaps the flow abruptly stopped, since giving and receiving are the same energy; and one cannot exist without the other.

Giving is not something to be forced. Giving comes from the heart, not from duty, to be well accepted and true. When a gift (tangible or intangible) is rejected, the receiver may not understand the circle, may not like themselves enough to feel deserving, may not love themselves, or may not be tuned in to the vibration of the awesome circle of giving and receiving (so not tuned in to you). It is not appropriate or helpful to force gifts, nor is it beneficial to take the rejection personally.

If it is you refusing to receive, notice why (*really* why) you do that. Have you been told it's a sin? Do you feel you need to always have a gift in return? If the latter is the issue, please remember that a smile and gratitude are sufficient and wonderful exchange.

Are you just a Giver? Giving is awesome. Notice, though ... do you take pride in trying to give more than anyone else, especially without receiving anything in return? If so, you may be stopping the flow. Do you not like yourself; are you looking for your actions of giving to make you look larger than life? At some point, your cup will become empty, and it could always be full when there is an exchange, and when you give to you and allow yourself to receive.

Do you receive when others give to you? If not, imagine how they are likely to feel and respond when you reject their kindness (it might be similar to what you would feel if someone didn't want to receive from you). This does not mean you have to accept all gifts; you may at least graciously accept the spirit of the gift. True gifts are unconditional.

Joy and abundance are the energy of which we are made. *It's all unlimited!* Imagine that. The more you receive, the more there is for others too! The more you give, the more there is to give! Think about that and then act on it. Tap into the unlimited abundance of this Universe!

Giving and receiving are the same. Feel the flow. Enjoy both; enjoy the circle. You may even give selflessly in one area, and receive in another (or to and from different people). As long as you joyously allow the circle to complete somehow, it works. You might do a nice deed for someone, and if they ask how to repay you, simply ask that they do something good for someone else (pay it forward). Accept their gratitude!

BREATHE AND AFFIRM:

I GIVE AND RECEIVE JOYFULLY.

Gratitude

Gratitude is a wonderful show of appreciation for every little and big thing in our lives; particularly when we've been asking for, praying for and/or manifesting a situation, an emotion, a thing.

Once you have that which you have wished and prayed for, do you hold that grateful feeling for long? What if it doesn't come to you looking like you thought it should?

How often have you received something you asked for, and your response has been "finally!"? How often have you received and it wasn't exactly as you expected? Did you gripe and complain? Do you feel you truly deserve what you asked for? Did you acknowledge that you were heard, at least in part? Were you specific about what you wanted? Have you thought that perhaps you've received exactly what you need in order to meet your request and continue to grow (you didn't really think you were finished with your improvements, did you?)? Be grateful anyway!

Be grateful for all that you want even before you have it. Gratitude is a powerful attractor. Imagine being grateful *as though you already have* what you desire or are manifesting. And be grateful for every little thing and person present in your life now.

Exercise for gratitude: Make a gratitude list. Think of three things (people, circumstances, feelings, yourself, etc.) that you are grateful for and speak this gratitude aloud or silently first thing in the morning and/or last thing at night. Add to this list daily. You will find a very long list! You will feel blessed, and you will attract more of what you're grateful for into your life.

From now on, say thank you (sincerely) every time there is the slightest opportunity. Expressing gratitude is an energy that will create more blessings and successes in your life and that of others.

BREATHE AND AFFIRM:

I AM SO GRATEFUL FOR THIS LIFE!

Guides

We each have Guides, and usually more than one type. Be in a good flow, and get into the habit of listening to them so they can really help you! "Tuning in" to receive information from your guides simply requires paying attention to different vibrations. Being open to sensing, hearing, seeing, feeling and/or knowing will help you to notice your guides. It's not a far place to go, and it helps if you are able to breathe and be quiet within yourself. Become open *without judgment* to whatever comes. Trust in the higher guidance and wisdom. You will know instinctively, intuitively, what the truth is.

The trick is to not second guess your Self, not to chalk the wisdom you receive up to imagination, and to not expect the ordinary. Sometimes clients who come to me for Psychic, Medium or Life Path Consultations will ask which guide the info came from; the answer is that it usually comes from the collective, from the highest source, as I receive in many ways at once, and one guide only does not hold all the keys to your wisdom.

Exercise for meeting your guides: Sit quietly with no interruptions. Breathe and clear your mind, open your heart and your senses. Surround yourself with a bubble of loving protection, and a silent statement that only Love can enter into your environment. Hold the intent that you are open to meet one of your guides at this time. Pay attention gently to what you hear, see, feel or know. You might hear a name or sound, you might get a glimpse, you might feel a presence, or you may just know something about your guide.

Whatever you receive, acknowledge it with gratitude and ask for more information for you, such as: "How will I know you in the future or what may I call you?" "What are you here to help me with?" "Is there anything I might need to know from you right now?" And wait a moment for each answer without concern for *how* that answer comes to you. Keep it rather simple at the first meeting, breathing deeply, so that you get used to each guide.

When you meet your individual guides, each can give you incredibly useful guidance, and will. The next time you do this exercise, greet the guide from last time, thank them, listen, and then ask for the next guide to appear. Your guides may be a combination of deceased loved ones, angels, elementals, ascended masters, old soul friends, or guides you haven't met before. They are of loving energy, and are to be loved, honored and respected. They have an important job to do for you! You are not taking them from anyone else, and you are never asking too much of them. They have agreed to do what they do, and they love it!

BREATHE AND AFFIRM:

I GRATEFULLY PAY ATTENTION AND LISTEN TO MY GUIDES.

Guilt

Turning guilt into gratitude is an option we always have. Take for example the wonderful lunch you had with a friend; did you enjoy it or did you feel guilty afterwards for being late, taking up too much of their time, too much of the conversation, or too much … ? When you pay attention to what you feel and do (or perhaps your lunch mate felt it), it's possible that you're also feeling respect for the other person's time, their attention to and/or friendship with you, etc. Whatever it is, how about turning guilt into gratitude, and gratitude into something spoken? Why not tell them how grateful you are, and then as a second step, make an intention that will keep you on schedule with friends, respectful of their time, whatever applies. Share your new decision with them (communicate it out loud!), and watch that friendship grow.

It's also possible you feel guilty because you didn't like your behavior (or this may be true of your friend if they are feeling guilty). Then it's time to look at your patterns and why you behaved in a way that you weren't proud of or that wasn't in integrity. If this is the case, fix it! Just the decision will make you feel better; much better than wallowing in guilt! Perhaps your religion taught you guilt; ask yourself, how is guilt loving? It's not.

Here is your permission to let go of guilt. We all feel it from time to time, but it is one of those negative emotions that we don't choose to keep. It can be toxic! It is a heavy energy, and thus gives us something to learn from, with the desire to create better circumstances and move on. And do learn from your circumstances before absolving yourself of guilt!

Think about it. If you are one of the many who feel guilty about even your whole existence, how can you learn to love and respect you (so that others can love and respect you) and to feel that you have something to offer the world? It's Your Life after all!

BREATHE AND AFFIRM:

I RELEASE GUILT, AND APPRECIATE MY LIFE!

Goddess / God / Great Spirit

Being intuitive, psychic or gifted in any manner doesn't have anything to do with religion! Where you have faith or who you have faith in doesn't matter, that you have faith, does; particularly if the faith is in something greater than this Life, in something greater than you, these bodies. You will see titles or references interchanged in this book, such as: Goddess, God, Gods, Great Spirit, Universe, All That Is, etc. All refer to Unconditional Love and Creation, and are interchanged so that it is known this is *not* a book on religion, and so that you can imagine the content of this writing may be true for everyone. All words are used in the highest faith and love.

Use whatever description you choose in place of any of these words when you see them in the book; remember that our language is somewhat lacking in describing All That Is, especially as interpreted by each of us.

As you learn to pay better attention to your own intuition, you will recognize (perhaps you already do) that as a Soul in a human body you are part of a larger flow of Love, Abundance and Wisdom. It is the awareness of this energy and paying close attention to it that translates into "intuition" or being "psychic" in some fashion. No religious background or affiliation is required, and as in all of life, there is no judgment of others for their religious preferences or lack thereof.

Perhaps our breath truly is Great Spirit or joy as the expression of our soul moving through this body.

BREATHE AND AFFIRM:

I FEEL THE LOVING CONNECTION TO SOURCE WITH EACH BREATH I TAKE.

HHH's

Happiness, Health, Healing, Hypnotherapy

*True happiness leads to health on all levels;
physical, spiritual, mental and emotional.*

Happiness

What is true happiness? How often are you happy? Be honest with yourself. Is it an emotion you experience often or easily? Imagine it as a primary emotion. What would it take for that happiness to be your life, your current situation?

Happiness is different than joy, although it is of that light vibration. Joy is what we are as souls ... unconditional love, before we come into these bodies and as we exist in them. Happiness is a human emotion (though it is of the joy energy) much more pleasant to experience than sadness, grief, or anger. Perhaps you're already a happy person. Yay for you! Keep it up! If you're not, how about making a decision that you'd like to experience happiness most often. Now, how do you get there from where you are?

Exercise for getting happy: Do you know what negative emotions you experience most often? Think about it, then allow an answer when you ask to notice what you're holding on to, that is attached to that emotion. Now decide to let go and heal from whatever it is (even if it means letting go now, and healing/learning later). If you notice that changing your circumstances will make it easier for you to stay happy, do it! It does not do you any good to hold on to any negative emotion or event. The past is history!

Learn from your emotions and your life experiences. No one else "makes you" unhappy, don't give them that power! If you are unhappy in a relationship, only you can decide to get happy or create another life where you will be happy. The future is a mystery, until you create a wonderful, happy one! And remember that Now is a gift, that's why it is called the Present. Make the most of it ... be happy!

Meditation is a great way to let go of stressors which contribute to unhappiness and dis-ease in the body. Nature will help if you'll go out and experience it. Happiness can fill that opening you're creating by letting go of the negative. Choose to wake up happy every day, and spread it around!

BREATHE AND AFFIRM:

I AM HAPPY NOW!

Health

Physical, mental, emotional, and spiritual health are all equally important. Do you pay attention to all aspects of your health? We are more than just this body that houses our spirit (spiritual health). Our bodies (physical health) come with a brain (mental health) and with emotions (emotional health).

Often in our busy lives, we get a bit lopsided, and focus on just one or perhaps two of these aspects of our health. Like a table or a chair with four legs, if even one leg (or aspect of our health) is neglected, it can become broken or shortened and will not support what it needs to. Stay in balance and pay attention to each aspect of your health in order to experience your best life!

Start with your inner health and well-being. When we are happy, joyous, it is energetically very difficult to become so imbalanced as to become physically ill. All is right in the world when all is right within you. Keep your thoughts full of radiant health and happiness.

Exercise for health: Affirm to yourself: "I choose to allow only radiant health!" If people tell you some disease is "going around"; rather than fear it, simply turn your thoughts to knowing your immune system is strong, know that you can take the necessary rest for yourself to stay in balance (you don't have to be "taken down" by illness or dis-ease), and that no illness can land on you! "I am surrounded by white light. I am radiantly healthy!" Focus on everything else joyous in your world. Remember that what you think about is what comes into being.

When we feed our physical body the nutrients it needs to continually boost our immune system, we feel better overall, and the rest of life is easier to focus on. Eat whole foods, grown on the earth, and get nutrients naturally in forms the body can easily assimilate. You'll find that the vitamins, minerals, enzymes and other essentials for our health are found in foods we eat; specifically those foods which have come from a live source; fruits, vegetables, fish, beef, etc. If you're eating something manufactured, imagine what's in it (a hot dog, for instance) ... most likely nothing of nutritional value. Lacking certain vitamins, minerals, enzymes, etc. can cause mental and emotional imbalances also. Supplements may be helpful, though maintaining a good balance through eating natural foods is much easier for our bodies to assimilate. Plant some carrots and munch at your leisure!

Choose health care practitioners who are skilled in and concerned with the Whole you for your physical care. In addition to allopathic medicine, look into acupuncture, chiropractic, iridology, herbalism, Ayurveda medicine, and so on. Be sure to find people skilled and loving their practice! And always choose the simplicity of eating well and keeping your immune system strong. True superfoods are a great source for complete nutrition ... these are foods that we can live on without anything else; there are only a few. I include a sea vegetable from an unblemished place of the ocean, in my diet. This way, I've given my physical body a head start; an essential daily boost, similar to the boost I give my spirit by meditating twice a day. There is more to life than being caught up with dis-ease of the body, mind or spirit! Feed you what you need on all levels so that you can live this life to its fullest!

Spiritual health requires something different for each person; find what works for you. It may be moments of solitude or silence each day, full of love and gratitude. It may be religious or spiritual activities. It may lie in communing with Mother Nature. Asking for wisdom each day and drawing an oracle card for the guidance may be your choice (follow that guidance!). Passive meditation is excellent for staying in balance. Any and all of these pursuits will help to satisfy spiritual health.

Emotional health requires paying attention, and perhaps keeping a journal. This way, it is easy to notice if your emotions are in control of you, rather than the other way around, or if you need to release them (and writing in a journal can be a good release). Physical exercise of any sort, dancing and yoga are great ways to process emotions. Remember that drama is a drug, and emotional hangovers are tough! You can choose to stay out of drama by intending not to create it, and by not engaging in it. The only emotions worth keeping are of joy and love!

Mental health includes getting out of your mind from time to time! Do something physical, listen to pleasant music, and pay more attention to your emotional and spiritual health to balance your mental health. If you're not already doing what you love for a living, it is often necessary to take a mental health day; a day for you. Imagine doing what you do love, and allow that to happen! Do things that do not require intense thought, such as movies, plays, symphonies, gardens and the zoo ... these are all great no-brainer activities. If you're not typically doing much mental activity, then by all means pull out a crossword puzzle, Sudoku, or a rubic cube to keep your mind strong! Remember that it is important to pursue what you're passionate about, and do that!

Balance it all so that you get in the habit of paying attention to you, and you will easily notice when and if you're getting out of balance in any of these areas. Seek radiant health on all levels! Be happy.

BREATHE AND AFFIRM:

I AM RADIANTLY HEALTHY!

Healing

Physical, mental, emotional, spiritual healing may all be paid attention to while in this body. Many of our society often focus too much only on physical healing or the relief of physical symptoms, while ignoring the likely sources of dis-ease; such as stress, excessive negative emotions and thoughts, and/or lack of hope.

Spend time to notice where you have been hurt, in which of these four ways, and then to spend time to heal You. This will help you to understand your Journey better, and to live it well. So many souls are living well past a hundred years on this planet now. If you're one of them, how healthy do you want to be on all those levels?

Many intuitives have the ability to heal others by a natural healing energy that flows through them, usually out through their hands. Hands-on healers have been written about throughout the ages, and have been called many things. Today, we still exist!

This is an ability that can be enhanced and channeled to help others, when a person so chooses. Perhaps you have and aren't aware of your healing abilities, but may be experiencing signs of it; consistently warm hands or tingling feelings, or feeling a need to place your hands on someone for a healing benefit. It is a matter of recognition of this gift and a decision to use it, at least for your Self. Become trained if you choose, remember to respect others' boundaries, and decide if you'll use it as part of your Life.

When combined with the ability to know what another is experiencing in their body (as a medical intuitive, such as myself will know), a healing intuitive can do much good in this world.

What I call a Medical Intuitive Reading (an MIR rather than an MRI ☺) will often uncover the emotional or mental source of a physical condition, as well as the condition itself. Usually the knowing will include where in the body the dis-ease is, and may include the emotions or circumstances that are the cause of the issue. The Flow of energy that will heal is always present when applied correctly. Seek the assistance you need to heal, we're here to help each other. Seek radiant health, and enjoy the Journey!

BREATHE AND AFFIRM:

I CHOOSE TO HEAL NOW!

Hypnotherapy

Hypnotherapy has assisted thousands of people in overcoming unwanted patterns and/or understanding their life lessons and life paths. It is primarily used for stress reduction, which is what you'll get no matter what else you accomplish, and is a tool you will always have, once you have experienced it.

All hypnosis is actually self-hypnosis, as it cannot be done without you and your desire and agreement to do it. The state of hypnosis is a very relaxed state where you actually continue to hear the words of the therapist while in that super-relaxed state. You will have agreed ahead of time on just what you're working on in the session, or what you hope to gain/learn from a past or future life regression/progression.

This is quite different from hypnotism, particularly in a stage show, where people give permission to "give up control" and take suggestions to do silly things without having to take responsibility for their actions. That's purely for fun!

Past life regressions and future life progressions are wonderful for understanding relationships we have in this life. Also, they help to shed light on why we do the same things over again (so we may finally learn the lessons and move on!). These regressions are painless!

It is in that relaxed state that we access memory, and just as memory of our early years in this life are available, so are memories of other lifetimes. It's just a matter of having the intent of what you want to accomplish in the regression or progression, and your soul will see to it that you remember the most pertinent lifetime(s) to shed the light.

With an experienced hypnotherapist, you will be guided to breathe throughout your session, through your memories, to remember all, and to release whatever is necessary to let go of. Since there is actually no time and space (that's just something we've created in order to have this particular physical experience), the other lifetimes you have lived are usually not in chronological order.

Although you can look up historically to validate certain facts from some of the lives you've lived, you will discover that you may have lived a life that overlaps another chronologically … a parallel lifetime. Or perhaps that you have lived a life in the twelfth century after a life in the eighteenth century.

The more important issue is what you learned during those lives, and the impact of the relationships you had then as carried into the current lifetime. You will discover that some of the souls in your life now also shared other lifetimes with you, though typically through different types of relationships. For

118

instance, your mother in this life may have been your neighbor or brother in another. You have been a woman as well as a man in other times; perhaps even a soul on another planet and/or in a different form. We have each been the abuser and the victim, hence the non-judgment ... just understanding of a greater cycle.

As you venture out to discover who you've been, you may find this life moves along a bit easier after understanding and letting go of the past.

Hypnotherapy is also an excellent tool for overcoming past traumas, whether from this lifetime or another, and for ridding you of old, negative and no longer useful patterns to replace them with new, positive, and perhaps motivational thoughts.

It is very effective to stop smoking, for weight control, pain management, and so on. Hypnotherapy is quite different than meditation; whereas hypnotherapy brings a very relaxed state, meditation goes far beyond to a heightened, calm state of awareness.

Hypnotherapy includes the idea that thoughts are things; very powerful creative things. The more positive thoughts you choose to have as new subconscious patterning, the easier and more powerfully you will be able to create your life now. A good hypnotherapist will help you to create what *you* want, with your goals and intentions in mind.

BREATHE AND AFFIRM:

I CHOOSE TO THINK POSITIVE THOUGHTS!

III's

Intention, IJK, Intuition, Imagination

*It is what you intend and imagine
that will come into Being.*

Intention

You are a powerful, intentional being! You intended to be here in this Life, after all. Now what do you intend? Do you intend to get up feeling happy and grateful in the morning? Do you intend world peace? Do you intend to gripe at your co-worker? Do you intend to be kind? Do you intend to cut other people off while you're driving? Do you intend success, creativity, growth?

There is no excuse for our actions; we act according to our intentions. Even if those are subconscious intentions, ones that we have by default ... the patterns we learned or even an off handed statement we made some time ago. When you decide you'd like to create a new and better way of being, it is up to you (and to each of us) to make conscious intentions; to be aware of what we are creating for our lives and in our lives.

An intention is different than a goal, although not separate from it. You might set a goal to complete a course of study in a particular amount of time. At the same time, you might set an intention to excel at your chosen field. The intention is often a way of life.

For *example*, if you haven't been paying attention to what you intend, chances are you are living from a pattern of intentions set by your early environment and family. Did you intend to do the work you do, or did you follow the patterns of your life? Whether it was conscious or unconscious, are you still choosing it and are you doing your absolute best at it? Is there another intention you would like to make?

Intentions will govern many of our thoughts; thoughts are things and they create our reality. We are each getting what we want at any given moment. Decide what you want, and intend it! Then read the chapter on manifestation to further bring it into being.

By living life in the way you're living it, you attract and repel people, circumstances, abundance, etc. When you pay attention, become clear, and make thoughtful choices, your life becomes intended, and is on purpose. Are you living on purpose, or by default? Are you taking responsibility for your life, or blaming others? It's up to you.

Remember that you, and each of us, have free will and choice, and you will become truly empowered when you set intentions **on purpose**. You will live your life on purpose. Intentions are personal. It is not for any of us to intend for another, ever. Intend to manifest all you've dreamed about, easily and joyfully.

BREATHE AND AFFIRM:

I INTEND TO CREATE PEACE IN MY LIFE.

IJK

We all have intuition, instincts, gut feelings. Yes, even you! Sometimes we explain it in fancy ways with technical words that are difficult to explain. But sometimes it's just something called **IJK ... <u>I Just Know!</u>**

What a great explanation of how we know what we know; from inside our gut, from higher guidance, from wherever it comes from. If you just know (energetically) something, act on it; share it, if it is appropriate. Your knowing doesn't need to be explained or defended, ever.

Imagine a life where you and those around you follow the rule of IJK. You would be paying attention to your gut feeling, your higher guidance, and trusting it. Then you would easily act on it. You may have a feeling to not get on a particular train, or to wait for the next elevator, and when you follow that guidance you meet a person you wouldn't have otherwise, or you successfully avoid a mishap. Perhaps you're guided to go to a different grocery store; you listen and consequently meet your soul mate.

Many years ago, I was driving down the street on my way to somewhere specific, and just as I was about to pass my favorite bookstore, *I Just Knew* I had to turn in and go into that store. Well, I had that familiar self-talk; I should go later ... why do I need to go in now ... maybe I just want to ... and then I stopped questioning and followed the knowing right on in the front door. As I did, I thought, "Now, why am I here?" Just then, a friend stepped out of a row of books and said "Ah, it's you! You're why I'm here." She knew and had trusted that she needed to be there at that time also; she *listened* and she acted! To make a long story short, she was a major player in this Life of mine, and in my Life's work. For her, I was someone she was told as a child she would teach a particular skill to. It felt absolutely correct for both of us independently, and we both trusted it. I am grateful to have listened to the "IJK"!

It could be something simple or something profound that occurs. When good things happen easily, why would you want to be attached to what you **think**, rather than the wisdom given you (the IJK or intuition)? Remember that you live in your body, with your brain; you are not your brain. When you are in alignment, you are wisdom and you can know wisdom; it goes with your spirit when you finally leave the body behind. Wisdom is what is true and is not separate from love. So, the logic the brain provides is useful for mental activity, but is not always a good guide for our soul's journey. To ignore the "how" is not what we've been programmed to do, though it is often in our best interest to set our intention and listen to the IJKs, never mind the how!

Hearing the inner guidance gets easier with practice and trust. Trust! Yes, we learn to trust our gut, our guidance. How often do you wish you had listened to You? The more often you do, and you take that leap, the more you will feel able to trust that guidance, the small inner voice that becomes loud!

BREATHE AND AFFIRM:

I AM SO GRATEFUL TO JUST KNOW!

Intuition

As a small girl growing up, I thought everyone simply knew everything about everyone else, since that was normal for me. When I discovered as a teenager that wasn't exactly true, shyness settled in for me. In later years, in asking why would a person need to know everything about someone else, the sensible and not so sensible answers that came included: **a)** we don't need to know, though all the information is always there, **b)** intuition or psychic abilities and knowing is as natural to everyone as breathing or walking, we just stop paying attention unless we exercise those muscles too, **c)** understanding others' plights may inspire compassion (WITHOUT JUDGMENT) for our fellow beings, and **d)** sometimes people ask us for a perspective on their life, and then we can share tactfully what we know for their benefit, **e)** if you're simply just always curious about other people, GET A LIFE!

Pay attention to your own life, your own lessons, and your own love. Stop judging others and practice kindness.

128

Even when we know something about others, we rarely know their whole story or what their life lessons are, or what their soul agreements might be; so we can simply offer kindness and compassion without judgment and perhaps soften or sweeten their journey a wee bit.

As we recognize who we are as intuitive beings, and we breathe in the joy of life, it becomes easier to notice what you know, rather than just what you think or feel with your physical senses. This book includes many chapters about various ways in which you might be intuitive. All are important, and paying attention to what you know and how you know it, then knowing what to do with that knowledge, is explained. The words "intuitive" and "psychic" are quite interchangeable, though some folks put a stigma on one word or the other ... remember, they're just words to help us communicate. Some folks call it a "gut feeling"; again, whatever is comfortable to call it is okay.

The more we remember to breathe, and to recognize the power of breath, the more connected we become to unconditional love, and the higher our vibration becomes as a species. We learn to trust, and intuition becomes common place again and is recognized, honored and respected.

BREATHE AND AFFIRM:

I ALWAYS PAY ATTENTION TO MY INTUITION!

Imagination

Use your imagination as often as possible! It will help you get out of any box you may have created for yourself. It is also a great tool to assist with changing your thoughts and your emotions, which will affect your reality. Your Life is exactly as you continue to imagine and think it is. What if you imagine it differently, and then change your thoughts to make it so? If you're happy with your life exactly as it is today, good for you! Simply enjoy it! Many people that I meet often don't like some things about their lives, and they just complain about it, and/or say that it is what it is and cannot be changed. Not so! Sometimes it is what it is, and you can change. Whatever the mind can conceive (imagine) and believe, it can achieve. Truly; try it!

Exercise for creating Your Life using your imagination: Sit quietly and comfortably. Breathe deeply and exhale, of course. Put a smile in your heart and know that all is well. Close your eyes as you imagine what you want; see it in your hands, feel it in your heart. Hold this until your heart and soul believes it. This is your imagination, so there are no limitations! The more you have of what you love and want, the more abundance there is for everyone.

As you open your eyes, feel the gratitude for being able to connect, imagine and create. Keep a thought with you all the time of this new reality, always releasing quickly any old thought patterns. Observe, as all you truly want comes to you.

Since we have created time and space to have this physical life experience, and everything is actually happening right now, it is possible for your life experience to shift immediately. If it does not, have faith, continue imagining, and know that you most likely have some experiences or lessons to complete as your new imagination comes to you.

BREATHE AND AFFIRM:

I IMAGINE WELL!

JJJ's

Joy, Judgment, Just do it!

Joy is the stuff of which we are made.
Strive to know a joyful center,
and Live from there.

Joy

When I had my first death experience, the best part is that I experienced pure joy and bliss on the "other side". At times, during passive meditation when I transcend my body momentarily, it is this Joy that I become. It is truly what we are; it is that ocean that we small raindrops return to and are never separate from.

So you can imagine that if you remember who you are, you may be in a nearly constant state of joy, and as a human being will also experience a full range of human emotions. Once you've remembered the joy, you may not want to allow the negative emotions to stick around for long! Why be unhappy, angry, or afraid to love for an entire lifetime? Why not be happy, joyous, and blissful? It's your choice as to how to handle your emotions (and only yours), how to learn from them, and how to share joy. Joy is empowering, and constantly experiencing it will help you to remain in the Flow of Life.

Exercise for making decisions to be Joyful, Excited and Empowered:

1. Make a firm decision on how you want to feel

2. Turn that decision into imagination and an intention

3. Decide to **BREATHE** throughout your day, triggering your intention (thinking, feeling and seeing it)

4. Notice your emotions and your actions throughout the day

5. Ask yourself: "Am I joyful, excited or empowered with this emotion/action?"

6. Notice your answer (**BREATHE**) ...

7. If your answer is "YES!" ... **BREATHE** and give yourself credit for being where you want to be ...

8. If your answer is "NO!" ... **BREATHE** and give yourself credit for noticing and change your emotion/action ...

9. Every time you notice yourself feeling joyful, excited and/or empowered; take a moment and **BREATHE** it in, giving yourself lots of credit for accomplishing just that!

10. Be grateful to You, and do this all over again as often as you want!

BREATHE AND AFFIRM:

I AM JOYFUL!

Judgment

Why do we judge? Do you realize how energy draining, time consuming, inappropriate, and destructive judging can be? Whether it's of yourself or others, it just complicates life. It doesn't do anyone any good!

Practice non-judgment. Start with yourself (you may like yourself better). Judging is different than assessing what or who is appropriate for you (correct or incorrect action). When you're tempted to judge others, look instead at how interestingly they have chosen to manifest their life, and how you don't have to live yours, or how you may want to use some of what you see in them in your life. Also look to see what is similar in yourself that perhaps you don't like (and then change it in you!); was that a mirror for you?

It is much easier not to put your foot in your mouth (by expressing your judgment) in the first place, than to have to pull it out publicly later. Most often, until we've walked a mile in their moccasins, we don't know the whole story of another's life. We are each so unique, each with lessons, some similar, some different, and we usually go through them at different times. We can learn much by listening and paying attention, with an open mind and heart, and without judgment.

Compassion is easier and has much more pleasing results, than judgment. Who are we to judge another? What measure are you using? Why would you want to? It only takes your energy and focus away from your own life. Are you much different or better than the ones you judge? If you feel your life choices are better than theirs, again wouldn't compassion and kindness serve both of you better? It just may lead to understanding. Get on with your life; don't let your precious time and energy be drained!

We never know the whole story about another, but can know more as we clear, step back, and allow the story to unfold, without judgment. Use empathy when interacting with others. Always use tact to speak the truth, and only when it's necessary and loving to speak it. It is as it is.

The field of unconditional love is the same as that of abundance; when you recognize and accept the love, you will have the abundance. Practicing non-judgment, having an attitude of "how delightful" or "how interesting" about all things, is a very clear and easy way to live life. It allows one to pay attention to what is most important in our own lives, without expressing harmful emotions to others.

This is not to say that we can't assess. Do assess whether someone in your life is supportive or destructive for you, and act accordingly without judgment of that person. Decide to stay in their life or not, and talk about it. Assess if your action is appropriate or not (do no harm) and change your action accordingly without judgment (learn the lesson and move on!).

When you find yourself judging, ask yourself under whose rules you are looking to judge. They are just your own. Who needs to comply with your judgment? Each of us has our own journey, and it is through that journey (ups and downs and not always in alignment with higher purpose) that we learn, grow and love. So, perhaps it's all perfect.

Go back to that place of joy, experience your own life, and make it easier on yourself and others by not judging. Instead, practice noticing what others do or say, and think to yourself "How lovely!" or "How interesting!" no matter what it is. This practice may help you let go of other people's stuff, and pay attention to your own magnificent life journey.

BREATHE AND AFFIRM:

I RELEASE JUDGMENT AND HONOR MYSELF AND OTHERS JUST AS WE ARE.

Just Do It!

In the famous words of Yoda, "There is only Do or Do Not." In other words, there is no *try*!

It makes sense! If you say "I'll try to meet you tomorrow", it implies that you might or might not make it happen. If you say "I will meet you tomorrow", you have set an intention and will make it happen (unless a rare something beyond your control happens). The former sentence tells us that you don't feel in control of your life, and/or are confused about what you want; perhaps you aren't able to speak your truth or set your boundaries. The latter statement says that you take control of your life, that you know what you want and what you intend, and that you co-create your Life! You do your best! Good for you!

Think of those two statements again. The first one is not likely to instill confidence in the person you are speaking to; their reaction to you may be quite different than if you made the second statement. Imagine now that someone said one of those things to you. With which statement are you *most likely* to feel important to the other person?

When you're breathing, when you achieve clarity, and when you have chosen to take joyful control of your life and speak your truth, life will work better for you. Other people are more likely to respond to you better (in a positive way). Just do it!

BREATHE AND AFFIRM:

I CONSCIOUSLY CREATE BY MAKING FIRM LOVING DECISIONS NOW!

KKK's

Kindness, Kids, Knowledge

*Be kindness, seek kindness,
and accept only kindness.*

Kindness

Kindness just might be the key to the best of this life. True kindness comes from unconditional love and is one of the easiest feelings and actions there is. When you feel and show kindness to another being, all animosity seems to float away.

What was the last act of kindness done for you? If the answer to that came easily for you, ask yourself how grateful you are for those acts of kindness. We don't want to become complacent or ignorant of the best part of life; the more grateful you are for kindnesses given, the more you will attract kindness.

The question is: what was the last true act of kindness you did for someone else? Do you easily make it a practice to do kind things? Do you practice random acts of kindness without expectations? That's a really fun thing to do! How do you feel when you do something randomly kind?

If you see neither kindness done for you or kindness you do for others, it's time to look at your life and make a simple decision. Your life is most likely not as wonderful as it could be. You can make the decision right now to be kind; practice at least one kindness a day. Even a random smile is kind enough. This is a stress-free decision! Just do it! Notice how good you feel (be careful though; it can be habit forming!).

Imagine the city or town you live in, and the drivers there. Imagine now if everyone decided to be kind while driving ... do you have a visual of that? Try small acts of kindness, let it catch on, and watch the world change. One driver, one road, one town at a time. So simple.

Imagine waking up each morning and thinking to yourself: "what a **kind** world I live in"! It may not be true yet, but this is a good start to create a kind world! What is your first thought of the day otherwise; anything productive or that feels good? Changing your thoughts is the first step to changing or taking control of your destiny.

Does this sound like a good idea to you? Have you made a decision to implement it? How about saying to yourself: "I'm deciding right now to be **kind** and to think **kindness** first thing in the morning". Beyond this decision, if you read the chapter on Intention, how about making kindness an intention of yours?

Now and then you may come across someone who doesn't know how to accept kindness at face value (do you?). When this happens, please don't take it personally, smile, and carry on with your day. We cannot force anyone to accept a kindness, and it would be counterproductive to do so. Know that you have touched another human in a positive way, and leave them with their journey; perhaps they'll ponder kindness too.

BREATHE AND AFFIRM:

I CHOOSE KINDNESS; I AM KIND AND I ATTRACT OTHERS WHO ARE KIND!

Kids

What blessings! No instruction manuals, though. We all started out as kids; remember that. Here's a simple way to remember as parents what your role is in their lives (or ... what you signed up for when they chose you!) ... always:

Love them!
Pay attention to them!
Educate them!
Nurture them!
Feed them!
Honor who they are!
Support them!
Be patient with them and you!
Praise them!

They're depending on you! Listen to them, and learn about them. To truly honor who they are, you may want some help finding out who they are; astrology is a terrific tool for this. All you need is their date, time and place of birth. Take it to a good astrologer to have a natal (birth) chart done. This will give so much information about what this little soul has come to Earth to do and be, as well as their primary personality traits. It's as close to an instruction manual as you'll get. While you're at it, have one done for yourself. A good intuitive can also give you some valuable information about them and their life journey! Write it down or record it; and learn how to nurture who they are here to become. Allow them their journey ... watch and simply (happily) guide them on it.

To love them means to do so unconditionally. To educate them means in all areas; it's no one else's responsibility, and if you engage others (i.e. schools) to assist with this, check in to see what other areas you need to complete this education in.

Remember that there's no such thing as failure; we can learn from mistakes ... failure is fertilizer, have some fun and wallow in it (you might learn from it!)! Allow mistakes from kids, show them how to do it better next time. Smile and be gentle with them.

Do always nurture them, and remember that during all the days, weeks, months and years that you are blessed with them, they are learning about life; if they don't do it perfectly in your opinion, be patient and teach them how, in the correct ways. Set gentle boundaries for them, and teach them how to do so for themselves.

They may be mimicking you; what a compliment! Praise goes much farther than blame does. Feed them in all ways; mentally, emotionally, physically and spiritually, and teach them how to feed themselves in these areas. Support them in all these ways also. Most of all, be aware, observe them, notice their strengths and who they seem to want to be; honor and encourage them (they do not need to be a duplicate of you, nor do they need to be who you wished you were). Honor whatever time it takes them to learn and grow. And then love them some more.

Please remember that you agreed to your life, as each child has agreed to hers. If you have not accomplished something in your life (or have), it is not up to your child to live your dream! You must help them find their own joy.

When you have kids or are a teacher of children, be sure to encourage who they are as intuitive souls. Give them a head start in this way, so they don't have trust or respect issues with themselves as they grow up. Remember that everything is possible and probable!

Do allow yourself quiet time to recharge so that you continue to experience joy and patience with your kids. As you lovingly give this time to yourself, you will teach your kids how to give it to themselves. Patience goes a long way, as does praise. Be sure to praise your child ten times as much as you criticize. These are precious, magnificent beings in the making. As you were and are. Be grateful for them!

BREATHE AND AFFIRM:

I LOVE AND ENJOY KIDS!

Knowledge

Knowledge is different than wisdom. Knowledge is what we learn in school, in books, or from each other; wisdom is gained through life experience and insight, and from the highest level.

How do you use your knowledge? If you know more than someone else about a topic, do you share it or do you gloat? Do you expand your knowledge, learning something new each day? It seems the more I know, the more I realize how much I don't know; is it the same for you? If you are a wealth of knowledge in a particular subject, share it; speak about it, teach it or even write about it.

Children are such a blessing; we were each one! They will grow and blossom as we feed them knowledge and wisdom; particularly when we do it in a loving and kind fashion. Some people learn best by listening, others visually, others kinesthetically; it's important to know how you learn, and how the children around you learn. By knowing this, it is easier to adapt and be patient as you either share or gather knowledge.

BREATHE AND AFFIRM:

**I GENTLY AND LOVINGLY
EXCHANGE KNOWLEDGE.**

LLL's

Love, Laugh, Live, Life Lessons

Laughter is the light of life.
Laugh well and often.

Love

What is Love? Is there a difference between Unconditional love; human romantic love; or love for a child? Do these conjure different visions; pleasant or even blissful, fearful, stressful or concerning? Still, Love is what it's all about!

Unconditional Love is what we're made of; it is the vibration of our Soul, our Spirit. It is Breath. It is what we are consumed in when we leave these bodies; it is the home, the place of our Spirit where we are all one with All That Is. The high vibration of unconditional love is such bliss that dis-ease and negativity cannot enter it, nor does the concept even exist. Many passive meditators rediscover that state of existence continually.

If you choose any single thing to do to improve your life, learning to meditate may be the best choice you can make. A passive meditative state assists in re-experiencing the natural state of unconditional love, consistently. An ensuing chapter is dedicated to meditation, so you can read more there about this potentially life changing practice that has been around forever. You will exist in Love!

Let's change tracks now, and talk about human romantic love. It certainly is a similar loving vibration, and though it comes from unconditional love, it is an entirely human emotion. Can you imagine being in a loving relationship with another, and having no conditions or expectations at all (as in unconditional love)? Usually not (did you laugh?). Romantic love is a blessing in our lives, although we always have some type of expectation around it, whether conscious or subconscious. It is how we learn.

To be taught about romantic love from a young age, about the emotions, the thoughts, the physical yearnings that go with it, would certainly help us open our eyes and perhaps pay better attention as we grow up and enter joyously into relationships. Through relationships we learn about us, and can be grateful, even in adversity, to those souls who've been mirrors for us. Understand the difference between this and Unconditional Love.

When romantic love attracts us, it can be a wonderful thing to enter into. In loving relationships we can re-learn how to enjoy and treat others. If you've had a relationship or two "fail" or "go bad", good for you! Check in to see what you learned from those encounters. Perhaps there is no such thing as a failed relationship, just one where two people grew in different directions, and it was no longer an appropriate interaction. Grow and improve yourself from this; allow love to enter in again.

Learn!! Love again! Laugh at yourself, and love yourself for surviving! Do not linger long; let go as you learn, and do not continually give up your energy for the past. You can't change it, although you can make a new future for you. And there are billions of souls on this planet; do you really think no one else will ever love you? Once you love you, others can and will. Learn from these relationships to love you and to like you.

All the while, strive to remember and embrace the unconditional love that you are!

BREATHE AND AFFIRM:

I AM PURE LOVE; I LOVE ME!

Laugh!

Laughter is the best medicine! It's true that we rarely fall ill when we're joyous and laughing! That smile gives your face value (and it takes many fewer muscles to smile than to frown). One form of Zen meditation includes laughing out loud as hard as you can for ten minutes, until your sides are almost splitting (metaphorically). Try it at home, or with your friends. The euphoria experienced afterwards is the objective.

Laugh at yourself (and you just may after that exercise!); laugh for the sake of it! Don't take yourself so seriously! Giggle first, if you must. Laugh with others (not at them). Laugh at Life itself. Spend time each day laughing; find something new to laugh at, even if it's just a bad joke. Be quietly "tickled" about something. This is essential to being a human being.

Laughter is a smile that bursts. Laughter can take the sting out of the air; it can reduce the heavy energy from too much thinking; and it can make the smaller troubles in life practically disappear. I don't know many folk who don't enjoy a good laugh, do you? It will improve the quality of your life, and extend it too!

How much of your day will you allow laughter in? Hopefully all of it! Imagine a whole day just trying to get that smile off your face, rather than remembering to smile ... sometimes reverse psychology works wonders.

BREATHE AND AFFIRM:

I LOVE TO LAUGH!

Live

Live this life well! Now may be all there is, so why not make the *absolute* most of it? This book is about breathing life in, and exhaling all else.   Understanding who you are as an intuitive being results in a Life worth living. We feel the flow of living best when we're paying attention at all levels, particularly intuitively. Then we become our best, and our best at living.

If there is some reason you don't want to fully live this life; seek professional help now! If you have fears about this life, it's time to look at them, and take steps to release them. Let love enter into the place where fear used to live; both create, and I promise that you want to create your life from love, not fear! You get what you think and feel about, so do you want more of the same, or do you want different? Intend your life, your kindest, most loving and magnificent life, now!

Pay attention to your intuition in all ways, and life will be easier for you. It may also be incredibly fun and abundant.

Make a firm choice to live this life for you. You made that choice when you came into this world; reaffirm it. Be grateful for it, decide what you want from it, and make it the best you possibly can.

Remember that we have chosen this Life; as souls, we have even chosen the timing for entering to our birth, surrogate, or adoptive families. Sometimes a soul begins the journey and "opts out" before birth; we know so much more at the home of the soul than what we remember here in our lives on Earth. It may not be appropriate to enter this life on many levels, so a soul may choose another time. So be it. Live the life you have, let go of control and judgment, and simply enjoy! Make it your best Life!

BREATHE AND AFFIRM:

I AM SO GRATEFUL FOR THIS LIFE!

Life Lessons

Why do we have life lessons? It may be that through experiencing this life and observing ourselves in it that we remember what unconditional love is, what self-love is, and how to always be in a state of love. It may be that we have lessons in order to experience the fullness of life on Earth at this time.

Whenever you feel stuck, or you continue to attract the same "incorrect" or "bad" relationship, or you're not getting what you think you truly want out of life, it's time to stop a moment! Review what you have attracted. Ask yourself if your intentions for this life are clear and strong; if not, make them so! Our thoughts and our intentions are intertwined, so be very clear with yourself. Thoughts are things, and energetically attract. Go back and notice what intentions you've been thinking about and acting on. What did you get? Was it exactly what you were manifesting by thinking about it?

Learn from these experiences; there are no mistakes! Be kind to yourself in this process … just notice and act.

If it is difficult for you to see in retrospect, seek a good friend or a professional psychic therapist who is intent on assisting you to find your answers without judgment. Talk openly about this life journey, and the progress you have made.

We want to be able to enjoy our journey, our successes, and all of our ahas! Look forward to being able to say more than just "Been there, done that"; let's add "lesson learned!" Until we do, we continue to repeat similar themes throughout this lifetime (and sometimes other lives as well). It's okay to get things as quickly as possible; though if you'd rather simmer and waste your life in self-pity and drag it on, that's perfectly alright too! Whatever you choose, remember that this is an incredible life that can be full of laughter and love; reach for it!

BREATHE AND AFFIRM:

I GRACEFULLY AND GRATEFULLY
ACCEPT THE LESSONS IN LIFE!

MMM's

*Meditation, Mediums, Metaphysics, Mud,
Music, Manifesting*

Manifest that which most sings to your heart.

Meditation

Passive meditation is one of the keys to your most joyful, clear and purposeful life. When we live in joy (where the word "enjoy" comes from) rather than fear, life works the way we think we really want it to, and passive meditation is one awesome method to re-experience joy.

Passive meditation is what I call the essential type of meditation, particularly for intuitives. It is that which we benefit most from when we do it twice a day every day for 15 to 20 minutes each time. It is different than a meditation you might practice to "get answers or inspiration", and is as different from sleep as work is from play. This passive meditation works with an intention of becoming so still for a moment that we focus on and remember only our soul, and are not aware (for a moment) of an existence that includes a body, mind or emotion. We will address active meditation later; it is most important for you to master passive meditation first, so when it is time and appropriate to practice active meditation, it will be easy.

Imagine a life where there is a constant noise like fingernails on a chalkboard, or a stuck chord on a musical track; life is then lived trying to block the noise and discord by ignoring what we hear and feel, and consequently running around like deranged chickens. Imagine instead being able to quiet those noises, and hear not only the blessed silence, but also our own inner guidance, laughter and breath. This is what you can accomplish through passive meditation.

Why, you ask ... Why not? What if life becomes easier once you have quieted yourself? What if you're truly able to know about your life without strain or stress, or asking another person? What if, with this simple exercise, you're able to reduce stress and experience bliss? What if, by meditating in this fashion twice a day every day, you automatically begin to carry a lighter vibration, a feeling of calmness, centering and joy throughout your day? What if you become more aware throughout your day? What if passion for your life and direction ultimately came more easily to you? (After, not during the meditation, that is.) Would that make it worth a try? So, without further ado, let's learn how. You don't need any props at all, however, if you'd like soft (SOFT instrumental only) music and a candle, go for it.

Exercise for meditation: Forget about your brain and logical (or illogical) thoughts, forget about your human emotions for a moment, and forget about the physical body. Got it? Doing nothing is productive!

You are Spirit, a Soul *in* a body *with* this mind and these emotions. You are not your mind, your emotions or your body. Focus a moment on who you really are (you as a Soul). After you've thought about that a bit, let's forget thought again, and pay attention to your Soul. Imagine where you came from prior to entering the body you inhabit at this time ... do you imagine freedom, ease, peace, bliss, joy, the absence of negative emotion? If you have not experienced these things yet, you're going to love passive meditation.

What you will need is the desire for peace. Loosen any belts, and sit down (loose clothing is nice as it allows us more easily to forget about the physical body). No lying down, as you are not attempting to relax and sleep, nor are you going into hypnosis! The intent is a *heightened* state of awareness of your Soul. Remember that if you hear phones ringing or dogs barking or otherwise normally distracting sounds, they simply fade to the background and might even facilitate you in removing your focus further from the physical. Be ready to enjoy this!

Allow your heart to have a smile slip in. Close your eyes (after you've read this☺), breathe in deeply through your nose (imagining a beautiful, clear, sparkling white light full of love) all the way down to your abdomen. This is your center. Now, blow out strongly, slowly and fully through your mouth, all the negative emotions and all the stress that has been stored there (it may be a brown or grey color). Do it again. And once more. Now, continue to breathe deeply in through your nose and out through your mouth. Leave your jaw relaxed and your mouth open a bit so that you no longer strain while breathing.

Continue to breathe deeply, as your inhale and exhale all become white light. Allow your breath to normalize on its own; the objective is a deep breath all the time (in between meditations also, so that you are always releasing stress and stressors). This is so simple!

Let's actually do it now! While meditating, here are **some additional tools** to get you to and keep you in a state of calmness and peace. Focus for a bit on the *color* of your breath ... perhaps it is golden or sparkling white, transparent even (see it). Then focus on the *sound* of your breath (hear it inside) for a while as you meditate. Next focus on what breath *feels* like, and then on what it would feel like to BE breath. Now focus on BEING BREATH. **Be Breath**. Experience Bliss. Repeat this as many times as you'd like; ultimately you'll find yourself as breath. Pure bliss.

As you were going into this meditation, you will have made a decision as to how long you will sit quietly for this meditation. Fifteen or twenty minutes is good. Your focus will simply be about your breath, which will assist you in re-experiencing You as part of the whole. As you notice (an inner knowing without thought) that it is appropriate for you to return to awareness of your body, gently incline your head toward your lap so that as you slowly open your eyes, you contemplate your hands for a moment before looking up. This is to "re-enter" your life here without sudden sensory overload.

This is one way to achieve the state of *being your soul* for a moment. Imagine that Spirit, God, Universe, Great Spirit, Goddess, All That Is, is simply an energetic field of unconditional love.   Not the human emotion of love, just Unconditional Love.   Perhaps that's what and who we are; unconditional love. When you hear of God within, or of being part of the Whole, etc., imagine that this field of Unconditional Love is like a beautiful, calm ocean and that each of us is a drop in that ocean; we have each chosen to experience this life in these bodies, but nothing ultimately will keep us from being part of that ocean. When we meditate, we can re-experience being part of the whole; it is possible to feel that absolute bliss.

As you embark on practicing passive meditation twice a day every day, remember that in the beginning you might experience right away what you set out to experience, or you might only get as far as feeling a lot better. Simply keep at it! The continual practice at about the same time in the morning and again in the afternoon will certainly take you to where you want to go, within. You see, there is no Where really to go, as wherever you may look, there you are! Do you see you? Feel you? Know you? Be still and you will. There is no such thing as time or space, really. We just use them so that we can have this life experience. So if we're quiet enough, we can transcend time and space.

Meditation of this type is as essential as sleeping and eating. It nurtures the Soul and brings a vibration to each of us that is higher and kinder. If enough of us remember who we are, we can bring joy and kindness back to this planet. Enjoy the enjoyment!

BREATHE AND AFFIRM:

I CHOOSE TO QUIETLY MEDITATE AND SOOTHE MY SOUL.

Mediums

There was a small psychic woman (barely 5 feet tall), who was arrested by city officials for violation of an antiquated fortune telling law. Somehow she escaped from the minimum security facility. As police searched for her, the newspaper headlines read "Small Medium at Large"! I have adopted this joke to retain the humor of who I am, and as a reminder to laugh with me (not at others ... we know better) as just a *small Medium at large*!

There are many descriptions and definitions of what a Medium is. Being a Medium is one form of being intuitive or psychic. Not all Intuitives or Psychics are Mediums. The focus here is on a spirit medium or psychic medium. The conventional definition of medium is the channel or the method to get information from one place, person or thing to another. Often you will hear of a person who communicates with the deceased, with angels, with spirit guides, and so on as a medium, such as me.

Sometimes the term is channel. The person who does this is akin to a PVC pipe, allowing information to flow through them. The information doesn't come *from* the person, just *through* them. It does not come from a specific guide, rather from the source of all things. At times, this source may be experienced by the channel as a "visible" group or entity, much more significant than a single guide or angel for focus purposes.

As a Medium I hear, see, and feel the deceased; sometimes they also identify themselves with a smell (such of certain flowers or old paint, perhaps a cigarette). Their personalities from this recent life on Earth show through so that they may be easily identified by the ones left behind. As I pass on what I receive, the person here (living) will know that it is indeed their loved one here to communicate. The messages from those on the other side may include love for the loved ones, and knowledge of where the living's life has taken them; they will often convey wisdom, and usually give solace.

There is no real death; it is simply a term we use to convey that the spirit has left the physical body. The spirit or soul has gone home ... moved on to the next phase of life. Where the soul goes to is a brilliant place, with unconditional love, bliss and wisdom. It is absent the physical body, the mind, and emotions. Can you imagine that state of just being? Observing from unconditional love with no attachments? If you have practiced passive meditation, you may have had a taste of what this is like.

Do you wonder or worry about your loved one(s) who have crossed over? Did they make it? Are they okay? These are questions you can ask of a Medium. Even though we each have the ability to sense those who have left, it is usually easier to sense for others than for ourselves. When people die, the soul leaves the body and goes to a marvelous, welcoming place. A loved one or two who have predeceased them (and often an angel or two) is present at the passing to welcome the newly crossing soul.

The life review for each soul is different, and lasts for different amounts of time, depending on how the life was lived … meaning did they get their lessons and accomplish what they came to accomplish. This is not an ironhanded judgment, nor is it punishment. It is merely the time for the soul to understand what was gained and what was missed in the lifetime as a part of the entire path of the soul; wisdom becomes apparent for them. The growth of the soul and the higher awareness of being part of the whole is the outcome. Time here on Earth is different than there; what may take hours or weeks here may be just a blink there.

A question that is often asked of me is whether or not children go to the same place as adults, and what about pets. Another is whether or not "bad" people go to the same place as "good" people, and if those who commit suicide possibly go to a different place. The answer is that we are all part of the same ocean called unconditional love, and as we shed our physical bodies (in any manner) we become aware again of being a soul that is part of this whole. So yes, we all go to the same place; we spend varying amounts of time in review, and we all regain awareness. And yes, the animals go there too!

Clients have come to see me to connect with a deceased loved one, or several deceased loved ones. When your intent is there for this connection, those loved ones are immediately right there with you, and through me. By the time the client is in my office, they often ask if anyone is around, and who it is. The answer is yes; and I'm always aware of the deceased, so many usually show up with you to be acknowledged. For me, it's like going to a party where I don't know anyone, but I see and feel everyone, and the one person I know (my client) asks me who's there. Well, I didn't know any of these people until just then, so we can go through each of them, or we can get to the person you most want first. You see, it works inversely for me, and when a client asks instead if their Uncle Joe is there, then Uncle Joe usually steps forward and gives his message; it's so much easier this way. Then the next soul and the next will come through and communicate as you desire it.

We all have the ability to be a medium or channel; some of us are just more inclined to listen than others (as some are more inclined to run marathons than others). Some are designed more for this talent than for another, and so do a service for others by paying attention to the information and sharing it with those who need and want it.

We use common sense, tact, and a sense of timing. For instance, I would not tap the person in front of me in the grocery line to tell her about her Aunt Bess who's hanging around with a message; the one in line may not be in a receptive place or mood to hear this; we always respect privacy and boundaries. Really, your loved ones are always around, and can be contacted by a medium most any time, so it's up to the living and grieving to contact the Medium. No props needed! And remember, being a psychic or spirit medium does not have anything to do with religious affiliations any more than being a rocket scientist or a bicyclist do.

When truth comes through you, it's unshakeable and feels correct. It is simple and profound at once. Do remember, however, that truth is often stranger than fiction. What is … is.

BREATHE AND AFFIRM:

I AM GRATEFUL FOR MY CONNECTION WITH ALL SOULS.

Metaphysics

Meta-physical ... meaning beyond the physical. This is an almost ordinary, interesting concept to ponder. Since we have established that we are souls with a physical body, a mind and emotions, perhaps metaphysics addresses anything that is beyond the tangible; which leaves the remainder of this life. Whether it belongs to this world or another is again not a religious thing; how we relate to it and what our perception is, is very individual, not to be judged, and is simply part of our experience.

So, when we talk about metaphysics, you can have an open mind, prepare for fun and interesting facts, and enjoy the journey.

Paying attention to many things beyond the physical can balance and enlighten your life. There is potential beyond your wildest imagination, and the energy of the possibilities is where it's at! Confusion may be put to rest as you also focus beyond the physical, and notice the signs and the knowing that you are given throughout your day. You will begin to feel more connected, and may then understand your Self fully.

Metaphysics is where we often lump ideas such as intuition, psychic abilities, ghosts and spirits, occult, witchcraft, etc. Anything beyond the realm of our five senses is metaphysical. Some folks will erroneously lump the eastern traditional healing modalities here, where they do not belong; such as acupuncture and herbalism. Remember that most of Life exists and happens metaphysically. Open your imagination and notice!

BREATHE AND AFFIRM:

I HAVE AN OPEN MIND AND HEART!

Mud

This is a chapter that could go as easily under the topics of anger, energies, or toxins. Mud might capture your attention best ...

Some of us see energy more easily than others, or simply pay more attention to seeing or feeling energies. To me, the energy of anger and the energy of stress look like liquid mud around a person, in their aura. It usually feels thick and heavy as well, just like mud.

So we're going to address **responsibility** for a moment; not just to what we think or feel, but also to our attitude and what we speak. Did anyone ever tell you to wipe the mud off your shoes before tracking it into the house? Well the same is useful for anger; wipe it out before going anywhere! If you are carrying anger around, or you're feeling it for any reason, remember that it is YOUR anger. No one else's. No one made you feel that way ... they may have pushed your buttons, but they're YOUR buttons. You can choose to get rid of those buttons, you can choose to feel an emotion different than anger, and you can choose to process or get rid of anger before you get it on anyone else! Do you really think you'd feel better if others were as angry as you? Are you in a state of love or even in your integrity when you choose to keep anger with you, and don't care if you get it on anyone else? Probably not! There is no such thing as "righteous anger"!

Certainly anger is a human emotion that most all of us feel from time to time. The trick is to notice it, deal with it, and get on with Life. The same goes for stress. Although stress is the largest creator of dis-ease, it usually instills a different reaction in us than anger does; still not a desirable one, and it still looks like mud, only not as dark or dangerous to others.

We are spirit beings having a human experience. You will experience a range of emotions. What you choose to do with these emotions is up to you. The most desirable of these emotions is love. The least desirable may be anger or fear.

Take a moment and take a breath. Imagine a moment when you were joyful or even happy; notice the vibration you felt. Was it light, pleasant? Now take another breath and imagine a moment when you were angry; notice the vibration. Was it heavier, chaotic, and unpleasant? Please take another breath and imagine a moment again that you felt peaceful or content. Nicer? Stay there! (Well, it is your choice, and the point is that you can choose to stay in whatever emotion you'd like). Optimally, you will choose the more pleasant, higher vibrational emotions such as love, bliss, peace, happiness, contentment. You'll make a much better imprint in the world this way, and will manifest better.

Now that you have felt the difference on several fronts of a few emotions, you might want to make an intention to always be experiencing a light-based feeling, and choose to bring that along as your essence and your aura.

There's a small chance that you want to choose to hold on to anger or even depression. If that is the case, perhaps you'll look to treat the depression, and remember what you're serving by living in anger instead of living in love. Your basis as a soul is love, so anger, fear, blame and depression are counterproductive to you. They will literally eat you up from the inside out. It's no one else's fault; yes your perception of all the events in your life up to today have helped to shape who you are, but you do not have to let the past hold and control you anymore!

Exercise: Make a decision to change or improve; a decision to move forward. Seek help if need be! No one has to go it alone in this life, even when you feel alone. Make the most of your alone time, and remember that You *are* love and You are loved! Make sure your decision is a firm one that you choose happiness, peace and ease! Then begin the passive meditation exercise in the "Meditation" chapter. As you go into your meditate state, decide to let go of everything negative in your thoughts, emotions and surroundings, and say softly to yourself "I choose to be happy now"! Begin breathing with this thought, let a smile enter your heart, and then let go of all thought. Plan on meditating every day. Be patient with you; you'll get there!

Now, let's get back to the mud. Do you take care with how you dress yourself; with what you wear on your physical body? Do you care because other people will see you? Are you hoping they'll see the best of you? Dress for you as though you do care. It's the same with the emotions we wear. If you would simply take stock just before going out the door, you will notice what emotion is on your surface. This is the story you're carrying for other people to notice. What's your story? Is it one you'd like everyone to know about? Will you feel better if people notice your simmering anger? If you do, you desperately need loving support and kindness, and can get that in a healthier fashion than by spreading mud. On the other hand, will you feel great if everyone notices the beautiful aura of compassion and kindness you exude? Most likely! So breathe in, deeply and well, all good things, and exhale all negativity before going anywhere!

It's your choice what your story is, what you wear, and how and to whom you communicate. Wouldn't it be lovely if everyone checked their baggage at the door! Save the processing and the understanding of the lessons for times of solitude. Work through issues with specific intent and with agreement from those assisting you, including friends who agree to listen.

Incorporating breath with clearing, cleansing and protecting yourself will help prepare you to walk out the door feeling good; feeling good about yourself, feeling responsible for you as you present yourself to the world, being peaceful and centered may be your new goal. Be sure to eat well, also; feeding all aspects of you exactly as you need … everyone is different. Sometimes what we eat or don't eat can severely impact our mental and emotional states, so check in and adjust accordingly.

As we go along on our journeys, perhaps many will come into awareness of this school of life. In that awareness, hopefully, is the understanding that we're each human, all going through our lessons. Hopefully understanding, compassion and forgiveness will abound.

Instead of bringing mud to a door, now you bring light and love. Do you feel better about yourself this way? Is it a more important story that your essence gives; one of higher purpose rather than lower emotions? Are you making the imprint you want on the world? You're doing great! Keep on!

BREATHE AND AFFIRM:

I SAFELY RELEASE ANGER AND MUD, AND I RESPECT MYSELF AND OTHERS.

Music

Play your music! Sing! Dance! Enjoy! Pay attention to the types of music you like; it's food for your soul, and can be a special vibration for you. And yes, for your emotions. So gravitate toward the beautiful sounds, and the sounds that make you laugh and cry, sing and dance, and put a smile in your heart. Feel good music and calming music have their places.

Be careful not to allow in those harsh sounds with ugly words and violent intent. These sounds do not nourish you in any way; they scar your being. Please remember that your tastes (and moods) may not be those of others. If you're enjoying your tunes, it's not okay to spike the volume so others have to feel and hear it ... they are most likely enjoying their own music (you wouldn't want their choices thrust on you, why thrust yours on them?). If you already get this one, good for you!

180

Allow the sounds that resonate with you; close your eyes for a moment and notice how different music helps you to feel the joy in your Self.

BREATHE AND AFFIRM:

I HEAR AND FEEL THE MOST
BEAUTIFUL MUSIC!

Manifesting

You create your life. You are capable of manifesting whatever life you imagine, whatever you want, and whatever you truly believe is yours. You will find tools to manifest throughout this book. Being in the Flow of Life, knowing who you are, loving and respecting who you are, finding quiet meditative times, and really imagining and intending the life you want will help you manifest it.

Remember that thoughts are things. What you think about, what you imagine, what you feel and what you visualize are what the Universe knows you want more of. Don't believe it? Look at what you do have, and how often you think about what you don't want … so you continue to get more of what you think about. Do you want to change your Life and manifest differently? Read on!

Exercise for manifesting: Decide what you really want in all aspects of your Life. Make a list of everything that comes up that you do NOT want; decide that you are going to manifest change and create new. So let go of that first list now; breathe deeply and really let it go. Now decide what you DO want. What do you already have that you are grateful for? Make a list of what you want; breathe it in with a smile! Imagine having it already, what it looks like and what it feels like. Be truly grateful as though you have it now.

Bring to your mind and your heart every waking moment what you do want, being grateful and smiling as you walk through this life as though you are living it as you imagined it. Remember that this is an unlimited world we live in; there is unlimited love and abundance. When you receive all that you want, there will still be more. As we begin the flow of abundance, it tends to show up everywhere!

You just need to know you, and spend time healing and understanding the whole intuitive being you are. The keys to manifesting are: staying in a loving state, having faith, knowing what you want, believing it's yours now, staying out of your head and away from the hows, and feeling gratitude.

Since abundance is of the same vibration as love, the more you manifest it, the better and more loving you'll feel ... and the more there will be for others as well. There is an unlimited supply of all things, so when you manifest for you, it does not take away from anyone else! Go for all you want; intend well as you manifest. Be sure to include with your intentions things like inner peace, self-Love, forgiveness, and awareness; then include all the smaller specifics you can think of. This is being on a correct path.

BREATHE AND AFFIRM:

I MANIFEST MY LIFE WELL!

NNN's

Names, Nature, Neighbors, Now

*Immerse yourself in nature,
and discover the truest you.*

Names

What's in *YOUR* name? Our names give us a powerful opportunity to build our self-esteem, create empowerment, manifest joy and well-being in our lives, and to reduce daily stress. It's time to get centered, comfortable and self-empowered with your Name! Love your name.

Exercise for name empowerment: First, take your first name ... find a wonderful, positive word that begins with the first letter of your name. Ahead of that word put "I am". For instance, if your name is Betty or Bill, you could use the word "beautiful" or "brilliant", and you would Breathe and say to yourself "I am Beautiful!" or "I am Brilliant" (or both!). Then take the next letter and do the same: "I am Energetic" or "I am Inspiring". Continue on with each letter, and as you do, take a nice deep breath, exhale, and feel the smile in your heart.

This process will help you to feel good about you, and will begin to override those old patterns that are not so positive! Do this every morning, preferably after you look in the mirror and great yourself with a "good morning!" Throughout the day, remember at least a few of these affirmations, and continue with your middle and last names. You'll begin to see your potential in this life, and others will see you in a wonderful light; as you treat yourself better (most always a benefit of this exercise), others will as well. Life becomes exponentially better.

We teach others how to treat us, so by believing in ourselves, and treating ourselves as though we are our own best friend, others will learn to treat us well also. When we love ourselves, then others can truly love us also. What more can we ask for? Always and only use positive descriptions of you. Let go of any negative thing you have said or inferred about you. You are a magnificent being; believe it!

BREATHE AND AFFIRM:

I LOVE MY NAME AND MYSELF!

Nature

We live on a most miraculous and beautiful planet. It is essential as we learn to take care of it, and in order to fully appreciate and understand it, that we spend time in nature.

To keep balance in our lives, being out of doors helps to be "grounded" or centered in our bodies, especially being intuitive and gifted as we are. It's as simple as going for a walk amongst the grass or trees, the sandy beach or the cliffs nearby. Listen and hear the sounds of nature; look and see the unique beauty around you; feel and sense the powerful quiet; and breathe a soothing breath of fresh, clean air. Exhale all your worries, put a smile in your heart, and let nature heal your soul. Be grateful for nature.

The farther into the city you live, the more important it is for you to make the effort to reconnect and then stay connected with nature. Avoid the negative, violent, and sensational news. Allow yourself only good and happy thoughts.

Imagine while you're out there, the greatest fairy tale that you would choose if you knew you could do anything at all in your Life, and not fail. Then take those thoughts and ideas and keep them with you as you go about your Life. Anything is possible, especially when supported by nature! Show gratitude for nature and planet Earth, and for yourself. Get into nature often, re-imagine, and watch your Life change. Feel the respect you have for nature and the life it gives. You will begin to care more for nature and our planet, and will become part of honoring and protecting this planet, easily and effortlessly.

BREATHE AND AFFIRM:

I SPEND TIME BREATHING IN AND OUT, WHILE CONNECTING WITH NATURE.

Neighbors

I am so grateful to have the most wonderful neighbors! They are loving, kind, aware and always looking out for each other. Relationships with neighbors give us another format for experiencing joy (en-joying), connectedness, and for learning about us. It gives us a chance to hone our communication skills, and to live with others respectfully on this planet.

Small town neighbors are especially blessed, I think. They can watch each other and their families and grin about these journeys we've chosen. Neighbors in towns that have difficult weather are especially precious; you can and do depend on each other during potentially life threatening weather. Knowing this, a bond of kindness often forms, and sharing is easy. We automatically watch out for each other, the children, the pets, and the land. I grew up in such an environment in Alaska, and am so grateful for it, as it taught me how to *be* a good neighbor.

It is interesting to watch neighbors in some larger cities, where the focus is so often on work and on self to the exclusion of others or their environment. There is sadness and emptiness when these neighbors don't take the time to know each other and receive the blessings that abound right in your front yard.

If you happen to be one of these neighbors who don't pay attention to your neighborhood, how about taking a chance and saying hello to the next neighbor you see? Find out a little something about them, and share something about yourself. Chances are you will have a lot more in common than you thought. Remember, there are no mistakes, and there are many blessings, especially when we do not judge!

Love your neighbors, and be a kind and aware neighbor to them! Be grateful for them. You just don't know yet where it might lead!

BREATHE AND AFFIRM:

I AM A GREAT NEIGHBOR!

Now

Living in the moment, in the now, is it. We created this life with time and space so that we can interact on a physical plane, in this dimension, but there really is no such thing. So now is all there is.

Why do you wait, and what are you waiting for? What is within your control and what isn't? Don't wait on things beyond your control (and please don't waste the now with worry!). Now is the time to imagine, to love, and to manifest all you want this life to be. Enjoy and have fun! There will be enough struggles coming your way for you to learn or remember what you came here for. So do learn, and then get on with your life right now.

What happens if you're afraid to take a breath because you're in the middle of a "crisis"? How long do you think you can go without breathing? Breathe now. Right now. Let go and you'll see solutions providing themselves. Remember that joy is your natural state of being, and that you exist because you breathe, now. You do not need to hold on to any crisis or drama. If you really need to present a solution or comfort to a situation, you will be able to do so *after* you breathe. So how about breathing and living NOW!

The past is gone, the present is a gift, and tomorrow is always tomorrow. Get up, show up, pay attention and tell your truth (tell it to yourself, and live it out loud)! Everything you do today is important, as you're giving up an entire day of your life for it! An entire day!

So get in the flow; remember that you have this body, this temple you created with that brain and those emotions, and yet you are a Soul. Honor your spirit and make the most of this day, this moment. Breathe now! Enjoy it. Live it now.

BREATHE AND AFFIRM:

I LIVE PERFECTLY IN THE NOW!

OOO's

On-Purpose, Openness, Optimism

*Being on purpose is the combination
of heightened awareness, great intention
setting, joy and trust.*

On Purpose

What does it mean to be On Purpose? Do you ever find yourself floundering and doing things that don't matter much, or that make you wonder why you did them at all? You're not on purpose if this is so.

When we don't set our intentions for this life, and we allow ourselves to get so busy that we don't pay attention, or we lose our Self to others; then we no longer show up or pay attention, and often find ourselves just going through the motions or habits of the day. We are not on purpose when these things happen.

This is Your Life. Show Up for it! Pay Attention!!! Speak your truth, or at least know Your truth. Intend to Live this life; when you do, you'll find yourself being On Purpose. Why do you think that you specifically chose *this* Life?

For instance, you may want to be the most joyful, balanced high school teacher possible. It may be your intent to connect well with and lovingly educate each of those teenagers who come across your path. As you truly intend this, you become On Purpose. Teenagers who need and/or want what you intend will be put on your path; you will know what to do and will do it on purpose!

If you are baking a cake, and you intend to bake a marvelous cake, you will most likely put the called for ingredients in, on purpose. If you're baking out of habit, don't want to, don't care how it turns out, are distracted from the task, or stop in the middle, your intended purpose is not baking this cake, and guess how it will probably turn out? That's right; it's anyone's guess, as you didn't bake it On Purpose. There has to be an awareness of purpose to what you do, for you to *be* on purpose and therefore to create just what you want. What are you on purpose about?

BREATHE AND AFFIRM:

I AM ON PURPOSE!

Openness

True openness involves the absence of judgment. Looking at the world through the wondrous eyes of a young child, without expectation and with the knowledge that anything is possible, will help you to become open.

Why do we want to be open? There is an infinite world of possibilities that may help you to live a more enjoyable or fulfilling life in ways you haven't dreamed of. Many people have developed a fear of the unknown, hence closing themselves off to the unlimited potential of marvelous occurrences. Notice if you have become fearful, shut down, or are simply not paying attention; you might make a new decision right now to let go of fear, open up and pay attention. Remember that no decision is a decision, so will you decide that it's business as usual, or will you be open to the unexpected?

Openness also allows an ease to discovering your intuition. Noticing how you receive information is more acceptable when you are open to endless possibilities.

Put your brain on hold and be open to accepting all that you've experienced that perhaps you couldn't find a logical explanation for, that someone else shot down as hokey, or that you didn't understand. Pay attention to the wisdom you gained from that experience; whether it is about you or anything else. Be grateful for the experience and for your own openness to accept. Watch as more beyond the physical or beyond the logical unfolds for you!

BREATHE AND AFFIRM:

I PAY ATTENTION AND STAY OPEN.

Optimism

Gosh, have I been criticized for being optimistic! Lots of people sure do like their misery and their belief that this world is disappointing; so they choose pessimism. With pessimism comes a belief that if the pessimist can't have it, then no one else should be so ignorant as to think they can. Pessimists have usually lost faith, the ability to manifest, and have lost kindness. Well I sure enjoy the benefits of optimism; it includes the unlimited potential of maximizing this life!

It is amazing how some people will just rain on your parade! If you pay attention to that, it's even tougher to remain optimistic. So pay attention instead to what you imagine to be possible, and surround yourself with optimistic folks who are supportive of you in all you want, and wish success for others. Jealously has no good use, and no place in your life; so don't let anyone in that practices jealously. There is no reason to be jealous of another, anyway, as we can each create absolutely any life we want; it never takes from another when we do. If you see a life being lived that you would like, create your own; be specific and optimistic about what you want, and let others continue on their path without your interference. Wish for success for others in whatever way they choose, and then you can be optimistic that you'll create success for yourself!

Practice optimism; be too happy to permit the presence of trouble or negativity. Be so optimistically strong that nothing can shake your peace of mind. Speak happily and of prosperity and positivity to everyone you encounter. Smile. Anything is possible in this moment! I choose to always be in such an optimistic and loving state of being that everyone I encounter always leaves feeling a least at little bit more joyful.

BREATHE AND AFFIRM:

I ALWAYS SEE THE BEST
IN OTHERS AND IN LIFE.

PPP's

*Prosperity, Protection, Prayers,
Psychometry, Past Lives*

*Life is unlimited, in joy and in abundance.
Live as you choose, and choose well!*

Prosperity

It's your birthright! What do you think about prosperity? Do you have it now? Is it a lesson you've learned in what you deserve or how to achieve? Or are you still learning it?

It is not necessary to live this life in lack; as a matter of fact it's simply a state of belief. If you think you are prosperous, you'll get what you think about! Are you grateful for the prosperity you currently experience (if so, good for you!)? Are you afraid of being prosperous? Are you uncertain how to get there?

Have you had an upbringing that says prosperity is difficult or is only for a few? What about an old pattern that says the desire for wealth of any kind is a form of greed? When you know that we live in a field of pure potential, that prosperity is unlimited, you will know that the more prosperous you are the more prosperous others can be as well. Everything is possible!

Hold the gratitude for your prosperity. Stay out of fear; the fear of losing what you do have. Love it that you always have enough, or even more than enough.

The Source, Unconditional Love, is a vibration that is the same as that of abundance. When you regain faith, or are grateful for the faith and connection you have, you will be in the Flow of Life. This is the flow of love *and* abundance. When you allow yourself to know this, you will rid yourself of any thoughts, feelings or vibrations contrary to it and will experience prosperity. Try it; think it, live it, and have faith.

BREATHE AND AFFIRM:

I AM PROSPEROUS AND I APPRECIATE MY UNLIMITED POTENTIAL.

Protection

Many Intuitives who receive information in more than one fashion may become overwhelmed if a) they aren't familiar with how they receive, b) they remain open to all information all the time, and/or c) they haven't protected against too much information or unwanted negative energies.

Do you feel wide open to every "psychic" sense? Do you take on other people's stuff? Are you not sure who you are sometimes because you can't sort out who's feelings you have? If you are also a "sponge", protection is in order (and making some rules for yourself in regard to this).

As an Intuitive, Empath and a Medium who receives in every way, I find it consistently important to energetically protect myself from many free floating energies, thoughts, emotions, other people's intentions, etc. I simply don't need to know everything about everybody all the time (or even most of the time)! It is difficult to "shut down" completely, and therefore I protect.

The exercise in the chapter on clearing and cleansing is applicable here. Clear and cleanse habitually if you are intuitive and feeling out of sorts, overwhelmed or lost. Follow this by protecting strongly with the intent of receiving only that which is important to you, and that which is generally helpful in nature.

Remember the Golden Rule, and in protecting yourself, do it without intent to harm anyone or anything. It is a loving thing to do. When you need protection or help, remember courtesy also as you think about whom can help you if you're unable to help yourself. Ask your angels (they feel no burdens!), or physically call your favorite earthly guide or intuitive for assistance.

Even the most well-meaning of people instinctively *think* of their favorite helpful Intuitive (me for instance), wanting help and advice during stressful times. I'm grateful for that! When this is you, please also pick up the phone and call (thank you to those who do)! Yes, I'm capable of getting your telepathic message, and when I do I can send you solace or assistance of some kind. Please remember though, that at any given time dozens of people (millions on the planet actually) are experiencing strife; and it's all important, and it's all felt. I can assist best when we communicate.

Perhaps I have chosen to assist you, and I'd like you to choose a way to receive support from me that bears in mind that Golden Rule. If only twenty people at a time are "sending" me (or someone else) their distressed emotions at once, can you imagine how that feels? Sorting it out takes tremendous effort and then sending out assistance even more; please remember that Intuitives also attempt to have their own lives!

Often, I have friends or clients whom I haven't seen in a while tell me that something major happened in their life, and they are upset that I didn't call them ahead of time to warn them or prepare them for it. They expect I'm always on the lookout, like a personal assistant, not realizing that one person cannot do that for a thousand people, particularly while protecting to achieve balance. How wonderful if it were possible, and I am grateful to be trusted by so many! The practice of balance as well as protection is important here to be my best and centered ... I have created a structure within my life to be on purpose and effective for you! So can you.

Sleep time, which we all value and need in order to function well during the day can be a vulnerable time for Empaths, intuitives, precognitives, and so on. So it is important to protect energetically before sleeping; not because we don't care, but because we each need to take care of ourselves before we can assist others. Have you been on a commercial airline flight when the flight attendant announces that in case of cabin pressure failure to don your own oxygen mask first before assisting others? This is the same principle; if you're in the process of passing out, you aren't any good to your child! Protecting is essential.

If you choose to do this work, it is imperative that you also choose balance and protection. The needed information always comes through, just not obsessively, when regulated. Balance and protect always, and you'll breathe easier ☺.

A suggestion for you as an empath, or as a psychic or intuitive on any level, even if you don't do this work for a living is to make certain agreements. For example, I make agreements with All That Is that I will do this work (because I love it); although since I'm in a human body, I choose to do the work during the day, and mostly during my chosen business hours. Life does happen at other times, to me as well as to you, and yet this is an agreement I have with Universe as a form of protection and balance. So, when my protection is strong, it does not bounce your energy back to you, just off into the ethers. In this way, I am protected always, and able to function at my highest and best at all times. This protection allows the most important information flow when most needed.

Another agreement to make when protecting, is to choose to give and receive courtesy. Most of all, please remember that you can receive all you need, a straight flow of unconditional love, directly from the Source, just as I do. You do not need to go through me or anyone else to reconnect with who you are. Keep your power! This is invaluable to remember; revisit the chapter on meditation for an exercise to reconnect. If you are Intuitive or Empathic, protect!

Some people use a bubble of white light (the Source) to surround themselves in, with impenetrable walls. I like to do this along with a strong intent such as "nothing unlike love shall enter here." That way Love gets in, I am always walking in Love, protected by it, and sharing it with others. Try it!

Time alone in nature will also give you pause to reconnect and recharge as just you. Use this as a base, then bring in joy and gratitude, while protecting with white light. It's easiest to protect after clearing, cleansing and centering.

BREATHE AND AFFIRM:

I AM LOVINGLY PROTECTED.

Prayers

There is only one true prayer for others that I feel is appropriate for a person to pray for another. That prayer is for whatever is for a person's highest and best good. We never know the whole story of another person, or their soul's journey, and are not in positions to judge what is best for another. When we hold the thought and the light of someone's highest and best good, it simply opens more Light for them, without conflict of their own wishes. If you're asked by a person to pray a particular prayer for them, okay, if you choose to honor their wishes for themselves.

Example of the possible effect of prayer: While Sara was in a hospital severely ill for a week, having a horrendous hospital experience, many people prayed for her (and she appreciated their love!!). Each of them wanted what *they thought* was best for her. Do you remember that we never know the whole story? Well, none of these people checked in to see what she wanted or needed before praying, so there were all kinds of prayers floating about on her behalf, consequently creating quite a bit of confusion.

One friend had prayed that Sara would be kept in the hospital a long time because she thought Sara needed the rest. Another prayed that Sara would be released quickly because she and others needed Sara. Yet another prayed that Sara would gain understanding of her traumas related to hospitals. Another prayed that Sara would lose the weight she thought Sara needed to lose while she was unable to eat. Yet another prayed that Sara would move on the other side to be out of suffering. And so on. These are just some of the prayers Sara was told about after her release, as we discussed her difficulties through this dis-ease.

One friend who knows Sara prayed the best prayer of all, "whatever is for Sara's highest and best good." Which prayers get heard do you think? All of them; and perhaps the ones that are not selfish and which intend only the best for the recipient, without judgment are heard loudest. Which ones need to be answered? Remember that we never know the whole story, and that to be a true friend is to listen to and to support our friends without judgment, especially when we think we know better than they do!

When we have loved ones apparently on the verge of transitioning to the other side, perhaps the only prayer at that time is also whatever is for their highest and best good. If they need a final struggle to complete their journey, it is not for us to prevent that, nor is it for us to hasten it for our own benefit. We can pray and open that unconditional love be remembered, and we can offer to be of assistance in whatever way they need us, and we can pray for relief of our own grief. But let's live our own lives, and not impose our beliefs or prayers on others; respect their beliefs and their journey without judgment. Let them go if it's their time; rejoice in their life if it's not. Be physically present for them and listen!

Practice kindness, grace and humility. Send unconditional love and support, and pray if you have to for the highest and best good for yourself and others. Prayers for the world, for kindness, love and compassion and for you to assist in bringing that here, is the highest prayer.

BREATHE AND AFFIRM:

MY PRAYERS ARE ALWAYS HEARD.

Psychometry

Psychometry is a form of intuition. It is the ability to feel the energy left behind in physical objects, and to know about that object and its history. Knowing such things as who touched or held it, where it's been, and the history surrounding it, can be gained through the practice of psychometry.

We each leave energetic imprints everywhere we go. It is relatively easy to notice the imprint of another in an object, as all things are energy, including the object. Have you ever gone to sit in a chair that someone has just vacated in a public place? Did you notice the energy left behind in that chair before you sat (were you paying attention?)? If so, were you okay with sitting down, or were you looking around for a different seat? This is a simple example of Psychometry, when someone has left behind their "stuff", and we know it best by touching the chair and its energy.

Exercise for psychometry: Jewelry holds energy well, and if you're quiet, clear and protect yourself before picking up a piece of antique jewelry for instance, you will feel the energy of the last person to wear it, or even of a person who wore it for a long time prior to that. As you hold the object, remain quiet and still; you will see, sense, feel or know the history of it.

Psychometry is fun to practice, and if you have a group of people who are willing, have everyone share a personal physical object by putting their object on a table, and one by one having each person pick up an item (not their own), and share what they feel, see or know from that item.

The person it belongs to can confirm the knowledge that comes in, without volunteering any information until the receiver has finished sharing. As you do this, remember for the one receiving to protect well, become quiet and centered, not to judge, speak the whole truth, and enjoy the process!

This can be a very useful intuitive tool, and is popular to many because it is tangible. Let your trust build as you intuit.

BREATHE AND AFFIRM:

I AM GRATEFUL TO FEEL
THE FLOW OF LIFE IN ALL THINGS.

Past Lives

Most of us have lived many lives, many times (past, future and parallel), and we come into this life without full memory of all those lives at once, or we would be nuts, completely unable to function well or learn in this one! You can choose to remember other lifetimes, however, past, future or parallel. Some of you may receive spontaneous visions or senses of other times you've lived, while some will have dreams of another life. Explore all those; don't discount them ... they come to you for a reason. Hypnotherapy, as you've read, can help with recollection as well.

If you find yourself fascinated with a particular place you haven't been in this life, or a specific past time frame, there is a good chance it's related to another life you've experienced. Pay attention, do a regression or progression, and remember what it was that inspired you in that life, and/or what it was that you were to learn in that life that perhaps parallels this one, or it might even give insight as to your current life path.

Some people who are psychic/intuitive get glimpses or more information of other people's past or future lives. It may come with a feeling of having known a person for a long time, even on first meeting. This happens often when soul friends reconnect. Here is another value of paying attention on all levels, breathing deeply, and connecting with that calm center you have; you may notice these encounters!

BREATHE AND AFFIRM:

I AM GRATEFUL FOR THE WISDOM FROM ALL MY LIVES!

QQQ's

Question, Quickly, Quest

Fulfill your quest by finding your joy within.

Question

Question everything with your mind open! Curiosity and seeking knowledge make this life exciting!

Questioning also allows a heartset that anything truly is possible. You've heard the saying that truth is stranger than fiction? It's true, and how fun!

You may not find right and wrong answers for your questions, just different possibilities and potential. You might find yourself set upon a path of enlightenment; although usually the more we know, the more we discover that we don't know.

Feel good about your quest for knowledge; as we come into this world, it seems that the wisdom of the ages escapes us, and we have opportunity to relearn and rediscover with a new perspective.

Have an adventure with questioning. Allow answers to come in unique ways; i.e. another individual may or may not tell you an answer to a question, although nature might reveal an answer to you or you may have an experience that helps you gain understanding to your quest. Enter into questioning without expectation, and enjoy the surprises!

Be certain of what you really want to know. Saying "I wish I understood how a person could (do, say, act ...)" will often create a similar situation for you personally to gain understanding from. Are you sure you want to understand, or is there another way to express your question? It may not be what you want to invite into your life! Stay in non-judgment, and if you truly want to understand something, question it, and experience will help you learn.

Be very specific with your questions ... what exactly do you want to know? Do not be ambiguous, rather think clearly and ask well.

Question your own intuition. How do you receive? What do you receive; what type of information? When does it come? By questioning this, you will be more familiar with yourself, and can more easily develop your own gifts and talents, while still trusting what you receive.

Be grateful for the experiences and the answers, and do pay attention to what you ask for ... you are a magnificent and powerful being!

BREATHE AND AFFIRM:

I AM GRATEFUL THAT
ALL MY QUESTIONS ARE ANSWERED!

Quickly

Just how quickly do you need to get started on Your Life? How about Now! Are you living your Life well, and in the way you want?

Do ask yourself what you're waiting on? Are you waiting on someone else? If so, ask yourself why, get a Life, and go for it quickly! They'll catch up if they're meant to. Is it fear of what the future may hold that holds you back? Well, that's just projection. Refocus on excitement, intend Your Life, and fear will fade away. Decide to go toward your life quickly, and then live it easily and well! Then take all the time you want in your Life, as you will be living in the Now.

If you have done some of the exercises in this book, and have discovered what it is you want your Life to be right now (or at least what you don't want), begin your intention setting today! Do your meditation regularly. Decide how you want to be known and remembered. If a child were to mimic you in all your thoughts, words and deeds, would you be proud or satisfied? If not proud, make the improvements in your life quickly!

Grab hold of Life and Live it now!

BREATHE AND AFFIRM:

I GRASP MY LIFE NOW!

Quest

Quests for insights, for joy, and for the fullness of this Life, are ones you may want to consider taking on. Questing for your Self as a whole and complete being, appreciating all your nuances, your talents, your compassion and your capacity for unlimited kindness may be ongoing for a lifetime. Perhaps you'll quest for a greater understanding of yourself, Love, this life or relationships with your family, friends and/or co-workers. Be on purpose with your quest, whatever its length.

Set your intent, or intend to discover your intentions, and set out upon a Quest. This can be something you do while you go about your daily life as it is now, or you can actually go somewhere in nature that is quiet and you can find solitude. Stay for as many days as you'd like on your Quest. Remember gratitude, be open, breathe and meditate. You will find peace.

If you haven't yet found what you're passionate about, quest for it. Spend days only doing that which you smile about.

When you smile enough, a laugh will burst forth! Pay attention and soon you will be immersed in laughing while doing something you absolutely love. And you'll love it whether it brings you money or not; you'll love it because it makes you radiant. And if you have intended to bring in abundance doing what you're passionate about, a way will open for that to happen. Joy and abundance are of the same energy.

Life is easy if you let it be. As you quest, rather than getting tangled up in the "hows", quest for your intention rather than how to get there. We are here to experience and share joy, passion and kindness. Practice them, enjoy them, and feel the lightness of possibilities in your life.

BREATHE AND AFFIRM:

I AM GRATEFUL TO FIND
AND EXPERIENCE MY QUEST.

RRR's

Relationships, Right or wrong, Respect

All interactions are relationships.
Honor each person you encounter as you honor yourself.
Treat each person as you would be treated,
and this world will be a joy.

Relationships

Do you sigh with pleasure with the thought of this topic, or did you just groan? Relationships are a fact of our lives. Whether it's a relationship with your Self, a relationship with a higher power, with a child, a sibling, a lover, a friend, an animal, a parent, or a spouse, it's still a relationship.

Through relationships we grow. There is no such thing as failure in relationships. That's right, no failure. Sure, things don't always work out the way we want or expect, but that doesn't mean failure. It means someone became aware; someone grew; someone decided to be treated better; someone moved on; or someone communicated either truth or lies.

Try looking at each relationship that ends or changes as finishing a class or course in college. What did you learn from it? You might not have liked the teacher! Sometimes our worst enemy turns out to be our greatest teacher. How is that? We often learn to love ourselves in relationships with people who don't respect us or our boundaries, who become abusive or uncaring. We all have limits, and when those limits are tested too much or for too long, we can finally say "Enough!" Then we take care of us. We see to our needs. We can seek that ultimate relationship with our Self. How graceful were you in that relationship? Are you satisfied or proud of your words and/or behavior? Learn and grow, and then let go.

And only then, when you love yourself and you like yourself (your own company), will you attract others who can and will love you and like you also. If you don't love yourself, how (and why!) in the world would you expect someone else to? We're not talking about arrogance; we're just talking about loving yourself.

If you have a choice to love you or to not love you, which one do you think serves you better? If Love is all there is, and we come into these bodies as Love for this experience, perhaps remembering Love would be most beneficial to our existence here. And to spread Unconditional Love rather than other things might just have an outcome that is most desirable! Relationships might flourish and become easier to communicate in. The relationship with your Self might just be more palatable, and even downright enjoyable!

We enter into relationships for many reasons. We are born into relationships. We feel a connection, we are attracted in some fashion, and/or we recognize the soul we are within the body. Be grateful for each and every relationship you have, however significant or insignificant you deem it to be. Even your interactions with the grocery store clerk constitute a relationship; and a customer of the grocery store clerk is a relationship too. Notice your behavior with every person you have interactions with, whether they're slight or ongoing. They're all important, and may just make a difference in someone else's life. Choose to always be gracious and kind and your interactions (relationships) will be easier. Be on purpose and kind in all your relationships!

BREATHE AND AFFIRM:

I AM GRATEFUL FOR ALL MY RELATIONSHIPS!

Right or Wrong?

Perhaps there is no right or wrong, just correct or incorrect action. Just as there are no mistakes, we can learn from all we do and from those things we deem as mistakes. We can choose our actions as well as we choose our thoughts.

Often, things feel correct to do at the time, and then later you might say "wow, that was wrong!" I suggest that it wasn't wrong; rather that you viewed it in retrospect and saw the light. You made a decision at that moment, based on outcome, on what not to do again. Now say "I get it!" And decide to do those life circumstances in a different way; that's part of our journey, to learn about us and life from those aha moments.

This is not to say that it's okay to engage in illegal or immoral activity, rather to always remember whether or not you are intentionally violating another's boundaries, doing harm or being ignorant of human rights. It is incorrect action to do any of the above, and so we have set moral standards.

The point is that we all make mistakes; so consider the circumstances, consider your behavior and whether you were paying attention or not, consider the probable repercussions of your words and actions, so that you may make better choices next time. Choose a higher perspective with all that you do; breathe deeply and often, especially before speaking or taking action! Be on purpose with all your thoughts and actions.

When you feel you've done something "right", something that had a wonderful, positive outcome, amend that to "correct" action. In this fashion we begin to move away from the feeling of competition, and from feeling "better than." Just congratulate yourself for doing your best, for being in the flow, and continue to stay in that flow!

It becomes much easier not to judge others when we practice this for ourselves. Please do remember that actions you make will be reflected back to you; so be sure to give what you'd like to receive! Smiles and joy always work!

BREATHE AND AFFIRM:

I ACCEPT THINGS AS THEY ARE, AND CHANGE MY LIFE AS I WANT.

Respect

In this society, I have seen many young people with polar opposite attitudes about self-respect. Either they righteously believe they deserve it, and are angry when respect is not showered upon them, or they have so little self-respect that they are attracting more disrespectful relationships to them, further shattering their self-esteem.

Patterns have developed over generations about the morality of self-respect, and the difference between arrogance and humility. An idea has been passed down that taking care of others before self is of the highest order; it's not! Just as on a commercial airliner, you (and each of us) need to take care of our Selves before we can truly care for others.

This means having a true and basic understanding of who you are. You might ask yourself throughout your day, through each thought and action you have, if you are respecting yourself simply for being you. Helping others is absolutely a respectful thing to do, until you help them more than they help themselves, or more than you help yourself even in the most basic way.

Selfless acts are marvelous; Mother Teresa did them well. Is this your mission throughout your life: helping others? Very few are truly like her. Most of us like to give of ourselves from time to time, and it feels right to do so; the point is noticing any imbalance. You have to have fuel in you in order to go about your day, especially prior to doing things for others.

So many people simply want to help others in general, and find joy in doing so. Most find after time that they are drained, tired and sometimes depressed, as they haven't had a focused or purposeful path for helping. Respecting others more than yourself completes only half of that circle of giving and receiving. Many people who seek help often seek help for free, or feel that it is owed to them; as the service providers fulfill that need, the receiver (the seeker) doesn't respect what has been given, as it has not been assigned a value, and they do not value themselves. So the giver possibly feels drained, and has no balance, no way to recharge, no proper exchange of energy; and the receiver doesn't gain as much as is possible. The lesson is to *allow* others to respect themselves enough to exchange something of value to them (usually money) in order to receive the true value of that which is in exchange.

Example: Your friend Martha has told you about Sally, an acupuncturist, who gives acupuncture for free. What is your first thought? Is it "great, I'll go right over – what do I have to lose", or possibly "She must not be very good if it's free?"

Either way, you aren't expecting any service of value, as she has placed a value of zero on her services. And you may not value yourself by saying "what do I have to lose". Another common thought, whether conscious or not, is that Sally must not think very much of what she does; she also may have no self-respect.

While it's honorable to help others, be careful of enabling them on the way. Respect yourself, and in doing so, others may learn by example. Do practice random acts of kindness, expecting nothing in return. Be kind to yourself also, and be in balance.

BREATHE AND AFFIRM:

I RESPECT ME; I LIKE ME.

SSS's

Self Esteem, Shoulds, Souls & Soul Agreements, Stress, Seers

Remember your Soul, and relieve the stress you carry.
Find Your Self reflected in other Souls you meet.
We are all on a Journey together.

Self Esteem

Are you suffering from low self-confidence due to low self-esteem? Make a decision to build your self-esteem now! Here are some techniques to help build your self-esteem.

Exercise for self-esteem: Center your Self by being still a moment, closing your eyes, and taking a deep breath into your Center. As you exhale, allow a positive thought about you to envelope you and a smile to enter your heart. Continue until it becomes easier.

Bring to mind positive things about yourself; things you're proud of or are happy with. Start with the small and move on the big. Remind yourself that you are a magnificent human being, and are perhaps moving into the fullness of who you are. Be gentle and positive with You. Whatever else may happen today, you have found your core and will choose to Live Your Life from that place of Peace. True Strength comes from here. Gentleness, Kindness, Assertiveness, and Love also comes from here. Thus begins the boost of your self-esteem.

Say "I'm perfect right now." Begin, new and fresh, to be how you really want to be.

Notice if you are acting according to your Intentions, or if you are simply re-acting to stimulus or others around you. When you *act in alignment with your Intentions*, Life becomes easier and you are able to manifest powerfully.

Only allow positive loving thoughts about your Self in. Always think the best of You. If a thought tries to enter about You that is unkind or undermining, let it go immediately, and replace it with a kind, positive, true statement. If others try to undermine you in any fashion; let them out of your life! Keep only those who are also growing, who know how to like themselves, and are kind.

Remember: it is You who is your best friend. You create Your Life. You are awesome, and can continue to be so when you pay attention to You and interact well and lovingly with others. Imagine once a day that anything is possible. Remember the excitement, rather than the fear. Take the risks when your Heart says it's okay. Enjoy!

BREATHE AND AFFIRM:

I LOVE AND TAKE CARE OF ME FIRST.

Shoulds

Let's just take all the shoulds and shuck them out the window; what do you say? Or should I? Should you? To what end? Should according to whom?

Shoulds generate feelings of guilt and/or obligation most of the time. Shoulds keep us away from what we do, what we want, what we need and from being on purpose. When I'm asked "what *should* I do about this situation", even though I may see a most beneficial course of action I will ask the querent to be more specific; i.e. do you want to know what would be the most financially or romantically beneficial course of action (and if so, for you or for someone else)? Or are you looking for a completely different kind of answer? When we know what we're really asking, and we have intended to be on purpose in our lives, then "should" rarely has a useful place.

Have you heard the mental chatter "I should have stopped at the store, I just didn't have time?" Feel the guilt oozing out of that statement? Let's change that statement to "I wanted to stop at the store, but there wasn't time. I'll go tomorrow." That represents taking control back of your life, and an ease of emotions.

Perhaps the example of having a thought of someone, and after that thought is the one that says "I really SHOULD call her to thank her ..." When this happens, notice if you get a heavy, sinking feeling ... do you? If so, take a moment when the first thought of that person comes in, close your eyes and take a cleansing breath, and FEEL that gratitude that may have initiated the desire to thank her (before the "should" thought came in). Now, bask in the joy of gratitude and notice if you'd *like to* thank her. If so, do it in that joyful, light spirit of gratitude! If you next think about whether or not you have the time, if you're already seeing her gone away, if you're imagining her not accepting your thanks, etc., then notice that these are negative, sabotaging thoughts. Get rid of them within 2 seconds! Go back to the wonderful feeling of gratitude and act on it, because you want to, not because you "should"! Watch your world expand in wonderful ways. Live in positive emotions and thoughts.

What **shall** I do? Indicates more thought, feeling and purpose than "should" which implies that you need to comply with someone else's ideas or that you are crossed between what you'd like to do, what needs to be done, and what social mores might dictate. Do you feel just a little bit decadent when you don't do something you "should"? As though *your* inner decision to do other things might have been the right thing?

Get rid of the shoulds! They only complicate and confuse life, have no good purpose, and get in the way! Imagine instead correct and intuitive action, which involves being in the flow of Life, with desire, gratitude and joy.

BREATHE AND AFFIRM:

I CLARIFY AND THEN RELEASE
THE "SHOULDS" OF LIFE.

Souls and Soul Agreements

Most of us as souls in the afterlife (or the beforelife) made agreements with other souls to meet up at certain times in this life to interact with each other to learn and/or to teach something. This agreement is not to sit down at a blackboard and spell it out, rather to learn through whatever form of relationships we enter into.

Imagine what strong love it took for one soul to agree with another to come to this life to work with concepts of Self Love and Respect; then to create acts of rage or violence until the lesson is learned? Yes, it's a very sad circumstance, and has become so commonplace that it is often ignored, or the perpetrator gets the attention and not the victim. Remember to pay attention; the one who is receiving the abuse is a victim the first time, after that, it is choice to stay in the circumstance. Learn quickly! Even if some others are here to learn from you, it's not up to you whether or not they get it. You are responsible only for You, your thoughts, words and deeds! This

239

means that you remain objective, do your absolute best to communicate well, and be an easy model of what you believe in, without forcing your beliefs or emotions on others.

Sometimes, people don't remember or care whether or not they are in a soul agreement with another person or situation. If you feel you are in a soul agreement with another who is unaware of it, please don't allow that to keep you stuck until they do become aware; learn and grow as much as you can, then release them *and you* to continue your journeys, if appropriate (and you will know if that time comes). Most likely you will encounter them again; don't hold your breath though, get on with your life!

Enjoy your interactions with other souls. We can each decide that we will take this journey with grace and joy. At this time on this planet, human beings are intuitive beings; we can remember that, stay in a higher vibration, a higher consciousness, and life will simply work better and be much more enjoyable. Laugh at yourself from time to time!

The potential for our species in unlimited! As souls on Earth, as we live and learn to communicate in the best way possible with our fellow souls here, imagine how incredible our communications might be with souls who have chosen to live on other planets. They've just chosen other forms of bodies to live in (or not).

You've chosen this journey, make the most of it! Pay attention and fulfill your agreements with others as aware and gracefully as you can, and you'll feel better about you. You may even come to understand and remember why you chose this particular life in this particular body, with this specific brain and these emotions. Be grateful to yourself for choosing well!

BREATHE AND AFFIRM:

I AM GRATEFUL TO GRACEFULLY FULFILL MY SOUL AGREEMENTS.

Stress

Too much stress is the #1 way to leave these bodies (it creates the top ten physical dis-eases, and consequent demise) and go back to where our souls come from! Stress is not pleasant! What stresses do you put on yourself? What stresses do you allow from others? This is a state of being that often encourages people to blame others for their stress; if this is you, notice what you are *allowing* in your life. You create your life; you are always getting exactly what you want by what you think and feel about. If you blame others for your stress, you're giving them your power. Who you invite into your life, where you spend your time (work, play, etc.), and how you live is by your choice.

If you have too much stress in your life, notice the cause, learn from it, and make a change! Meditate, walk in nature, and use any or many of the other tools in this book to relax, breathe, balance and regroup. Let go of stress. Breathe it out!

If you say it's not so easy, that may be true for you at first, as it may be habitual; you can either leave things as they are, or create a better, easier life for you. And PLEASE don't care more about others than yourself! You can make changes for you, and leave others to their own lives! You will want to do this with grace, style, integrity and respect, and without taking control of other people's emotions (they will feel whatever they feel as a result of your actions ... let them!). Imagine the stress free life you want, and go for it! Now!

BREATHE AND AFFIRM:

I AM STRESS FREE AND JOYFUL!

Seers

A Seer is someone who has visions or intuitively "sees" upcoming events, or "sees" within another. It is another name for a type of Intuitive, and a name that was much more common centuries ago. The implication of the name is certainly gentler and more specific than "psychic".

Crystal ball gazing used to be a very common practice; a Seer or Seeress would align themselves and gaze into the ball to "see" or "scry" the answer to a query or the future of an event perhaps. Seers do not always need a crystal ball to see, however.

As a Seer, we are *shown* that which we need to see, and only that; we still live this life, and there is still a wonderful, mysterious journey to explore. If we knew absolutely everything, what would be the point in living this life? So we use the wisdom and the gifts we have been given to their fullest extent, and by doing so, know more than if we rely on only our five physical senses.

You may consider that a Seer is a wise one, who looks, sees, knows, and shares. If you are one, life may become easier for you if you use the tools set forth in this book. For scrying, practice by sitting in front of a clear or reflective surface, such as water (a small bowl may be fine); breathe, clear, center, and protect. Relax your mind, focus on the surface, and allow images to enter. A seer will have images, random or sensible, come in. Much practice allows this to become clear, and more understandable. As with many intuitive practices, it helps to speak with someone else to clarify what you have seen.

Open your mind if you believe yourself to be a seer, and practice! Be sure not to judge, jump to conclusions or think too much! Take what you see at face value. Ask for guidance when you need to know what to do with what you've seen; you'll receive it.

BREATHE AND AFFIRM:

**I AM GRATEFUL TO SEE CLEARLY,
AND I TRUST WHAT I SEE!**

TTT's

Today, Thoughts, Truth, Telepathy

The truth is what you know,
a belief can be shattered.
Truth is simple and undeniable,
with no need for defense.

Today

Today, this moment, now is all that matters. Who and how are you today? If this is the only day you have, what are you going to make of it? Will you breathe during the day? Will you show kindness? Will you do something magnificent? Take a risk or two?

Do you know what is so very important to you that if you have only one day left to experience it, you'll actually live it? Don't waste it!

Remember that time and space is simply our illusion so that we may experience this life. So as you live today, truly experience it as though you will sign your name to it.

Once again we remember that yesterday has truly past, tomorrow is a mystery, and today, this moment, is the only now there is. Are you happy in your "now"? How will you live this moment, your day of yours?

BREATHE AND AFFIRM:

I AM GRATEFUL FOR TODAY!
TODAY I LIVE!

Thoughts

Thoughts are things. Let me repeat that: THOUGHTS ARE THINGS! They are energy. We are not our thoughts; however what we choose to think about helps to create our reality. Every moment, you have a choice as to what you think about and how you think about anything. It may take some undoing to change the way you think if you've had a pattern for a length of time, so that every new thought you think is positive and happy.

There are multitudes of ways in which to change your thoughts. The first, most important thing to do is to realize what kind of thoughts you are having, what kind of thoughts you *do* want (make a firm decision!), and know that you will create a better life this way.

Do you realize that your life is exactly as you've created it? That you are getting exactly what you want? If you don't believe it, look closely and deeply at your thoughts, and you will see that you are and have been creating what you think about. Have you ever seen an event or a relationship and said "I really want to understand that?" Guess what happens next? You get the same or similar circumstance so that you can understand it. Choose carefully your thoughts and what you wish for, especially when it's emotionally charged! You can truly think and feel your life into being exactly what you intend!

When clients come to me to understand their lives and the events they've created, we always look at their underlying belief system (b.s.), what their thoughts are, and what they truly desire (their intentions). Then they choose to change, and change their thoughts. Here is where positive thoughts and affirmations come in to play (and action), and they are powerful. Think them and believe them!

BREATHE AND AFFIRM:

I THINK POSITIVE, BEAUTIFUL, ON PURPOSE THOUGHTS!

Truth

The truth is that the truth is easiest to remember! Rather than a belief, which can be changed, truth is. Make it simple on yourself. As you question and explore, notice what FEELS like truth. If you're uncertain, it may not be true and that's okay. Just notice.

Be truthful; to yourself first, and then to others. If you want to live your best life, this is a way to know where you are in life, why you do, say and act the way you do, and being truthful gives you the best opportunity to decide if you want to continue as you have been, or make changes and improvements along the way.

Have you ever told a non-truth because you think the other person wouldn't handle the truth, or wouldn't handle it in the way you hope they could?

If so, first remember that you are NOT in control of another's emotions (it's not okay!). If you disagree with this, ask yourself why you want to control what anyone else thinks, feels, experiences. Then I would ask you to get a life of your own; and pay attention to your own thoughts, feelings and experiences (enjoy YOUR life).

Second, remember that the truth may set you free! You may always tell the truth *with tact*, of course, and recollect once again that we don't know the whole story about someone else, and they will benefit in the long run by being able to know your truth and handle it however they choose. You, meantime, may let go and live your life. A truth told in love will run its proper course, and you do not have to dictate what that course is. Truth is about living the easiest and least complicated life.

Truth is not to be confused with unburdening yourself, or seeking absolution so that you are not responsible for your actions. It is about sharing the truths that may otherwise stand in the way of movement or growth. Always see truth for yourself, and live your life with your eyes truly open and seeing the wonder of possibilities!

BREATHE AND AFFIRM:

I RESPECT MY TRUTH, AND THE TRUTH OF OTHERS.

Telepathy

It happens all the time! You think of a friend and the phone rings; guess who? We get on the same "wavelength" with others as often as we like.

When you intend something and intend it strongly for yourself, and another person intends for themselves in the same fashion, the telepathic channel is open and you'll find both of you aware of each other on that energetic level. If you follow your Flow, you will most likely find yourselves in the same place at the same time without physical communication.

Telepathy is becoming even more commonplace, accepted and used. You can have a lot of fun with it and become proficient, if you practice. You may want to choose a good friend and decide consciously to do this together.

Exercise for practicing telepathy: Talk verbally and decide that you're going to meet at an undecided place on a particular afternoon, without setting a time; just that you want to spend an hour together, for instance. When that afternoon comes, you will each think of the other ... one or both of you will think of a place to meet (i.e. a café, a bookstore, your home) and suddenly you'll both be there at the same time. There is a possibility that unavoidable events happen that day that will cause a delay or canceling of the meeting, as life continues to happen. You'll know that too. If that is the case, it's still alright to pick up the telephone and chat! Give each other praise for "hearing" and following the telepathic messages. Do it again, and the more often you do the more proficient you'll become. It's easiest if you're in the habit of quieting yourself and finding your center.

Trust the process, and have faith in others that they will trust and listen also. Imagine what a nice pace our lives could have when we're all paying attention telepathically.

BREATHE AND AFFIRM:

I TRUST WHAT I KNOW TELEPATHICALLY.

254

UUU's

Universal Laws of Love

**The Universal Laws of Life are indeed the
Universal Laws of Love, as
Love is what we come from and what we are.**

Universal Laws

Laws are not something we usually think about when we think of the free flow of energy, the vibration of Love, and all things metaphysical. Over the years however, Guidance, and the Council of Light, has shared with me the Universal Laws (as in LAW ... **L**ove, **A**bundance, **W**isdom). Listed here in no particular order, these laws are such useful guidelines to make life easier and more harmonious for all of us. Practice them if you choose, and watch your life become kinder, wiser, easier and more fun!

THE EMPOWERMENT OF UNDERSTANDING AND LIVING THE UNIVERSAL LAWS

Awareness of these simple laws and the Intent to live and practice them creates simplicity to let go and live well. Here are a few laws to remember:

Practice non-judgment

Know the difference between judging and assessing for your own good. Do it kindly. Remember that you may not know the whole story, and trust what you sense. As you assess your situations and your environment, lovingly imagine that which you wish to create. This extends to you and Your Self; assess rather than judge, and make changes. Be kind to you.

Center, Cleanse, Protect

Enjoy you! Take a moment at least twice a day, every day, to breathe in to your center, and breathe out with a smile. As you do it again, do it with your intent to center, cleanse and protect You. You may follow this into your passive meditation, or do it after, your choice. Breathe and connect with your highest Self, with All That Is, as your constant objective.

Allow, Trust

Allow knowledge and intuitive information from all your senses; trust what you first know. Open the valve of information flow, and share what you know *as* it becomes appropriate. Trust the source, find that faith, and get out of your own way!

Welcome your Intuitive Flow

Appreciate who you are and notice how you receive, without having to prove it! Practice intuition in the ways most familiar to you; remember that this is normal. Notice if you're also an empath or medium, or if you see angels, guides or auras. Nurture you so that you are always in the flow of intuition, the field of pure potentiality. Remain neutral, kind and understanding of others. Explore, be open and advance in many types of intuitive reception.

BOUNDARIES & PERMISSION

Pay attention to and honor your boundaries and those of others. Whether you agree with others' boundaries or not, when it comes to sharing information you receive, notice whether or not you are crossing a boundary (or someone's privacy) if you were to share in the moment at that place. You will be intuitively encouraged when the timing is right, and discouraged from sharing when it isn't. Honor this. Ask permission when you are driven to share. Remember that other folks' lives are for them to live; always ask permission before gathering or sharing information about anyone else. When you share knowledge, *let it go!* Respect yourself and others. Set your boundaries and honor them in yourself and in others. Get a life! Receive info as it comes, and go about your wonderful day.

ALWAYS BE THE ENERGY OF LOVE & LETTING GO OF STUFF (WHO NEEDS IT ANYWAY?!)

That Breath of Life is the energy of unconditional love. When you breathe (and do it often!), remember this. The smile will come from your heart, bubbling into laughter, which is what reminds your face to smile. Always breathe, always be Love. Make it your intention to let go of all negativity with

258

every breath. Remember that worry only takes your energy and does not resolve anything; it does not prove love either. Make it your intention to feel and be Love every moment. Allow the ease of Life. Be the truest You; be like a rainbow with so many pleasant colors and energy after a cleansing rain. Without struggle, we wouldn't learn, grow and glow. Rainbows usually come *after* the rain; like letting go of the struggle to shine.

THE TRUTH DOES NOT NEED TO BE DEFENDED

Love just is. Truth just is, and you'll feel it, sense it, see it or hear it. Walk your talk, and never mind if others get it or not. We all have a right to *believe* anything we want; though when you *Know*, your questions will slow down or stop, because you have found Truth. You may not know everything all the time, though you can be in the flow enough to know enough. Live and let live; there are many paths.

KNOW WHEN TO SPEAK, WHEN NOT TO SPEAK & CONFIDENTIALITY (COURTESY)

Taking a breath accomplishes so much. Breathing in to your core taps into the place of blissful calmness and joy. Breathe before you speak, which gives the opportunity to know whether or not it's appropriate to speak at all at that moment; breathing keeps us from "blurting out" whatever comes to mind. Breathing in and out reminds us to follow Guidance, and to adhere to a personal code of honor. The empowerment of Awareness takes us to a higher vibration, so that the information shared is important. We remember that all of us have the ability and the opportunity to be whole, intuitive beings, kind and loving.

THERE ARE MANY PATHS.

Each of us may choose our own. Observe and allow, and expect the same from others. Remember this in communications with others. Learn from observing other paths.

YOU ARE JUST A MESSENGER.

You may intuitively receive all types of information; always remember that you simply pass it through. Do your best to be accurate and compassionate as you do so. Ask for guidance to assist with imparting the message lovingly so that it might best be heard and understood by the person it's intended for. Then let it go. The messages are not to be judged by you. We all have free will and choice.

PSYCHIC KNOWLEDGE IS NOT A RELIGION.

It is simply a flow of energy. Psychic or intuitive knowledge is simply something that flows through you, and through every being. Notice it and honor it. Use it or not, with trust and without judgment.

KEEP BALANCE IN YOUR LIFE.

Doing so will allow you peace, understanding and enjoyment in your life. Balance allows you to more easily incorporate intuition into daily living.

IT'S ABOUT THE JOURNEY.

We do not need to know all of what's ahead for us. Most often it's simply about experiencing and enjoying the journey.

SPEAK TRUTH.

As it comes in, speak the truth as you recognize it, especially to yourself. There is no need to judge it, be sure the listener is ready to hear, and certainly use tact. There is a smile with each truth.

THERE IS NO SUCH THING AS WRONG OR RIGHT.

Everything simply is. There is that which we learn from; either to do or say again your words or deeds if the result is positive, or to not do or say again your words or deeds if the result is negative. Learn as you go, and pay attention to your correct action!

YOU NEVER KNOW THE WHOLE STORY.

Particularly as an intuitive being, you will often receive information about others or a situation which gives you an "aha" of recognition. This does not mean you know a person's whole soul story; there is far too much soul history, and more to your own life than to know everything about another soul and their journey. Remember non-judgment, and that you are just a messenger. Practice kindness with all for whom you are a messenger.

LIFE IS EASIER WHEN YOU LISTEN.

So much will not have to be repeated when you pay attention and listen as a habit. You have two ears and only one mouth for a reason. Listen with your heart and soul as well. Listen to your intuition in all ways, openly and without judgment. You will hear what is for you to hear.

ANYTHING IS POSSIBLE.

Truly anything within your imagination is possible, and then some. Seek endless possibilities, fearlessly. All of life is miraculous.

THOUGHTS ARE THINGS.

Thoughts are energy, and therefore creative. Watch your thoughts, and create well! As you speak your thoughts, pay attention to your words.

BREATHE AND AFFIRM:

I TRUST AND PRACTICE THE UNIVERSAL LAWS WITH GRACE AND EASE.

VVV's

Vibrations, Voices, Visions

Open your awareness and the knowledge and vibration of all things will make sense to you.

Vibrations

You feel vibrations in music; and you may notice the vibration, energy or feel of many things throughout your day. Emotions and thoughts are vibrations. Colors are great examples of vibration. Vibrations are the dance of energy.

Exercise for noticing vibrations: Imagine your favorite color, close your eyes, and then imagine what it feels like to be that color. Then do the same exercise imagining the same color bolder, and then softer. Notice the different feel. These are the vibrations of that color and its variations. Another exercise to notice vibration involves stones of different types from the earth. If you pick up a rose quartz, hold it in your hand, close your eyes and breathe, as you quiet yourself you may feel the energetic vibration if this stone. Comparisons make it even easier, so pick up a different stone, a different color, such as a jade or obsidian. Do the same exercise and feel the vibration of that stone.

Everything has energy, a particular vibration, including you! As you become more aware of the vibrations around you, you'll discover that vibrations can tell us about other properties associated with them. The stones in the examples above, for instance, each have qualities about them that assist with healing in specific fashions. Rose quartz, you may feel, lightens the heart with self-Love. Although this may be its main property, some people may feel a vibration somewhere else in their being where the energy of this particular stone may help as they hold the stone. The more often you practice feeling and accepting vibrations, the easier it will become, the more aware you'll become, and the better you'll feel.

Emotions have energy. Negative emotions usually carry very heavy or chaotic vibrations. Positive emotions will carry lighter, more pleasant vibrations. Recollect that like attracts like, and pay attention to which emotions you carry most of the time, and what your vibrational field is sending out to others. Notice vibrations with all things. This will lead to a heightened respect for all life, and for yourself as you begin to see all of who you truly are, and who we each can be.

BREATHE AND AFFIRM:

I EASILY RECOGNIZE AND
HONOR VIBRATIONS.

Visions

Visions can come at any time, day or night. They can be pleasant or not. Do you have visions? Do you ask for visions? The ones that come unbidden, especially about something that has not yet happened, are often prophetic. They might also contain information about or for someone else.

If you receive visions frequently, it will be a good idea to write them down, discuss them with someone else who honors their intuition. Then make room for the rest of the knowledge to come in. You may receive further instruction as to what is intended to be done with the knowledge you've been given.

A form of intuition is through having visions. Sometimes they can be as clear as a movie or subtle as a dream. They might be vague or blurry, until you've given it practice. When they appear unbidden and suddenly, it may be because you are in a relaxed state.

Visions are sometimes the clearest form of intuition, as we have been trained to trust our eyes. This is your inner or intuitive eyes seeing. Trust it!

BREATHE AND AFFIRM:

I TRUST MY VISIONS.

Voices

Clairaudience is the ability to clearly hear voices from beyond this physical plane. It is not the most common form of intuition, though it may come sporadically to any intuitive, and comes frequently to a few.

The voice or voices may be soft, or a simple loud voice with a message. Often, you will hear a psychic say they "heard" a message; this is usually not an actual voice, but rather a telepathic message. It is just as powerful and important either way. The important thing is to determine how and what you're hearing, if you are hearing voices.

I will quite often hear a voice with one word describing the essence of a person I've met in my personal life. Words like "strong" or "trust" or "fun." As years have gone by, these words have been highly accurate in summing up that person as they relate to me.

It is common for a strong voice also to be heard in times of impending danger; that which has been called the small inner voice, or the voice of God/Goddess or Great Spirit, becomes the large inner voice, and actually audible at times. Practice listening within through breathing and meditation exercises and this small voice will become noticeable and easier to distinguish; whether you hear it telepathically or as a voice.

BREATHE AND AFFIRM:

I RECOGNIZE THE VOICES OF LOVE,
AND TRUST THEIR MESSAGES.

WWW's

Weather, Wisdom, Work,
Wise Women & Wizards

*Wisdom comes from experience,
open mindedness, and stillness.*

Weather

The weather around our planet is changing almost daily (in case you hadn't noticed). Major destructive forces have increased in frequency and intensity. Lives have been touched and devastated immeasurably.

As we take responsibility for the damage we constantly do to this planet, we can intend to treat Earth with kindness and love as we intend to do so with each other. As long as bombs continue to be set off under water, underground, and from the air, and drilling into the Earth occurs in inappropriate places and ways, and so on; the tectonic plates will continue to be jarred, and the cumulative effects will result in, at least, major earthquakes that not only change the topography of the land, but that take souls with it.

As other acts of violence occur around and to the planet, weather patterns will continue to change and intensify. The vibrations of the negative actions cause undetermined damage.

Many of you reading this today feel weather patterns, whether you're aware of it or not. Often (certainly not always) migraines are caused by intense weather (pressure systems particularly). Left or right side sinus pressure often indicates a high or low pressure system moving into your environmental region. A frontal centered headache indicates a stationary front for many people. A severe, persistent neck ache often indicates significant precipitation coming in. Inexplicable and sudden dizziness may indicate either hurricane/typhoon/cyclone energy or earthquake activity.

As odd as this may sound, if you experience any of these symptoms and are able to match them to the weather, simply acknowledging and honoring this and then taking a deep breath with gratitude for the forewarning will usually alleviate the symptoms. Let me know if you are in this group, and we will have a discussion group to take this wonderful awareness to another level.

When we practice awareness of and kindness to this planet, and we remember that all our physical nutrition is supplied from the Earth, life will become much easier.

Our bodies will be healthier and more cooperative, therefore making it easier to stay in emotional, mental and spiritual balance.

Breathing exercises, as explained in an earlier chapter, may be expanded to assist in this worldwide healing of weather patterns. You'll also feel better!

It is possible to affect weather with thoughts; collectively we can focus on calming the weather or even bringing rain if called for. Some of the cleansing (such as with rain) is necessary; however we can positively affect the planetary weather with current and long range thought, combined with awareness, to move us more gently and gracefully into the Shift.

Earth's varied weather climates affect each of us differently. Take note of where you live, and whether or not you love the weather. Are you healthy there? Do you crave a different climate such as desert or ocean or mountainous?

If you have experienced better health or general well-being in a climate other than where you live, it may be time to consider a move. Appreciate the Earth's weather, live in it, take care of the Earth, and be where you want to be!

BREATHE AND AFFIRM:

I AM GRATEFUL FOR THE WEATHER ON THIS PLANET, AND I CHOOSE TO TAKE LOVING CARE OF THE EARTH.

Wisdom

Wisdom is wonderful. It is beyond knowledge. In our world, as we know it, wisdom is a combination of knowledge and experience. We can get to wisdom quicker and more easily if we listen to the elders, and if we listen to and take in Guidance.

Whereas the gathering of knowledge may have caused us mental anguish (or not), the gathering of wisdom is light and freeing. When people die, they go to the Light, the place of pure Love and Wisdom. When we successfully meditate with intent to transcend this world and these bodies, we connect with a place of wisdom and can know that wisdom.

Hypnosis can create a relaxed enough state to assist a person in doing what I call a Soul Journey. In this journey, rather than going to another life time, the Soul momentarily goes beyond physical death to "home", to the Source. It is easy to hear or experience wisdom in that place, and the wisdom is always simple and profound. It assists, when returning, in remembering to allow the small stuff of your world to be small, and to focus on what's truly important in life.

Seeking wisdom can make life much easier to live on purpose, and with intuition! Become wise is a great intention to make, as it means we integrate knowledge with our Life experiences.

BREATHE AND AFFIRM:

**I GRATEFULLY ACKNOWLEDGE
AND ACCEPT WISDOM.**

Work

Work ethic ... is it a current topic or a thing of the past? Let's make it essential again, as it has everything to do with integrity, kindness and awareness.

If you have a job working for someone, practice gratitude. Stop complaining! Just as you were looking for a job when you found this one, so your employer was looking for an employee at the same time. My guess is that the business you work for would rather have a grateful and pleasant worker who believes in and promotes her business than someone who only shows up to collect a paycheck, as this becomes counterproductive to the business. Think about whether or not you are creating the life you really want. If so, go for it and be grateful! If not, be grateful as you go forward!

Check in with your Self again. Are you feeling stuck and slinging mud? Are you happy doing what you do, or is it time to get happy doing what you do? Is it time to do whatever it is you are doing much better so that you can be proud of yourself, or is it time to do something entirely different that perhaps you Love to do?

Whatever you choose to do for your work; Love it! Spread kindness and compassion while you do it and smile from the bottom of your heart! You will make an enormous contribution to society with just that simple act, and you'll feel better about You. When you love what you do, it no longer feels like work!

BREATHE AND AFFIRM:

I LOVE MY WORK AND I EXCEL AT IT!

Wise Women & Wizards

Listen to your elders! Listen to those who seem to know, especially if you are looking for answers. Those who know themselves best, know how to get out of their own way and have wisdom and insight to share.

Wise women and wizards who are willing to share what they know are gifts to us all. Listen well, and learn. Take whatever feels like truth for you, and discard the rest (discard, not discount).

Life experience, an open mind, memories from other lifetimes, and a strong connection with All That Is beyond this physical existence helps to develop wisdom. These folks practice and honor the Universal Laws, or similar beliefs, and live lives of their own rather than meddling in those of others.

There is a general belief of Unconditional Love and the common good. They use their talents to advance our society, and to spread compassion.

You may be a Wise Woman or Wizard, or on your path to being one. Either way, remember clearly the ways of the world and how to stay out of your own way. Remember who you are, and how you have agreed to be.

BREATHE AND AFFIRM:

I RESPECT WISE WOMEN AND WIZARDS
AND THE WISDOM WITHIN ME!

XXX's

X-ray

Examining one's Life by looking thoroughly within without judgment, will result in the possibility of re-making one's entire Life.

X-Ray

People often ask if my "knowledge" of others has to do with X-Ray vision; it does not, although it is similar in that what I see is beyond the physical (meta-physical). It includes the physical body which I am made aware of (primarily from the inside); I see people's auras before I see their skin colors, and I see the energetics of their emotions and mental state, which are rarely hidden and are usually the cause of physical dis-eases in the body.

Advice is then given to share with the person I am seeing on how to correct the emotional and mental issues, and ultimately the physical issues. An MIR (medical intuitive reading) rather than an MRI is what I call this, when I see health issues within a person.

Contrary to popular belief, I do not walk around reading minds; nor do I ever know your whole story ... none of us ever know the whole story. As you become proficient with your own intuition, and more varied circumstances present themselves, you will understand why not judging is so important.

Information is given to me that you need to know; it is then shared with you, and then I let it go. There is so much information about everyone, that if you or I were to try to hold on to information about others, we would be completely overloaded, and would have no room left for our own lives! To keep that information would simply lead to drama, gossip or rumors; we do not know the whole story, and we need time to focus on the creation of our intentions. So let it go!

I will give you all the loving advice and guidance that comes through for you; and it will! Nothing is held back. There are no deep dark secrets. It's all illuminated for your review, not mine, and always without judgment.

You may actually be able to "catch" thoughts in the energetic field. This does not mean you are "reading" all of a person's thoughts. Please assure them or yourself of this! We all have privacy, and respect that of others.

BREATHE AND AFFIRM:

I LOVE WHO I AM,
AND MY JOURNEY IN THIS WORLD.

YYY's

Yes!, Youth

Possibilities are endless.
Saying yes when it brings joy to your heart
will bring those possibilities into reality.

Yes!

What a marvelous, powerful, positive word! Yes makes all things possible. Do you say yes very often throughout your day? Yes to receive all things good for you? Do you say no when you mean yes? Pay attention. Get what you want and deserve. Say yes to you. Yes, thank you.

The vibration of this word is positive, light and highly charged; so different than it's opposite. While you are consciously intending your Life, focus only on all that which you will say yes too; only that which you desire. Let's intend all things, and that our Universe is unlimited in its potential, yes?!

The exception is when your intuition tells you NO! Then listen, and say no. Be sure to distinguish between your intuition and possible fear; using the guidelines in this book with help you stay in the flow of intuition, staying there will allow you to be excited about life and embrace all its possibilities. You'll want to say yes to Life!

Everything may be a miracle, yes?! Do you want to try new things? (Yes is the answer!) If you want to be aware of all things, all you have to do is say yes; then open all your senses, take a deep breath, and exhale. Expect a miracle.

BREATHE AND AFFIRM:

I SAY YES TO LIFE!

Youth

Ah, the ongoing search for the elusive youthfulness! It's internal, you know. You're only as old or as youthful as you feel and as you intend. Perhaps you are a youth.

Youthfulness is different than being childish, of course. Having a childlike wonder and feeling refreshed, healthy and happy most of the time is the idea behind wanting youth. Appreciate the wisdom you have gained, and be in awe of the world!

Exercise for feeling youthful: Pay happy attention to all aspects of your being, let go of learned negative patterns and thoughts about you and your body, release fears (don't accumulate new ones) and enjoy life! Continue to accomplish these things by spending time in nature, breathing intentionally, having fun and meditating.

Use your imagination. See yourself in your minds' eye as you'd like to look and feel. Remember the feelings you have/had when you're playing; encourage spontaneity in yourself. Appreciating our young folk, observe and guide them, and be grateful! Let go of the small stuff, and see simplicity.

Young people, who have been incarnating in the current generation and the last one, are nearly brilliant! They are highly intuitive as a group, and are aware that this world is shifting. It will behoove all of us to nurture and further educate them, to listen to them, and perhaps to follow their lead. Become youthful, and imagine the possibilities!

BREATHE AND AFFIRM:

I AM GRATEFUL FOR MY YOUTH, AND I AM GRACEFUL WITH MY SELF.

ZZZ's

Zen, Zest for Life, ZZZ's

**Balance in your Life includes the
quiet as well as the zest for Life.
Experience in awareness all of Life.**

Zen

Such a feeling and a state of being is Zen! As we go about our busy lives, what is sustaining is the ultimate feeling we allow ourselves in the flow of all that is. To be "Zen" is the opposite of being active and doing; rather, it is a state of being quiet with exhilaration, being in the vibrational flow from where understanding and wisdom reside. It is also a place of bliss where one can let go of the need to make things happen in a particular fashion and time. It is a wonderful experience to frequently visit to keep the small stuff small and to stay out of stress and worry.

Laughter is a great way to accomplish Zen. Have you laughed until your sides feel like they'll split (how long ago?)? When you finally finished the laughing bout, did you feel cleared out and free? And was there a ridiculous grin on your face, while nothing much mattered? What a marvelous experience ... and an emotional, spiritual place to be! Do it again, and do it often!

The state of Zen, however you accomplish it, is as important to our overall well-being as sleeping or eating properly. It promotes health physically, mentally emotionally, and spiritually.

Imagine incorporating it into your life. Does that feel like a special gift, or almost too good to be accomplished? Well then, do it! You deserve it!

BREATHE AND AFFIRM:

I JOYFULLY AND EASILY PRACTICE ZEN.

Zest for Life

Zest ... Feel it. Live it each day, as though this day is your first, or your last one. Make the most of it. Sign your name to everything you do (not literally, of course). Be You, live large, make a statement.

Since you are in this life, you can choose how to live it and how to create it. You can do it in a fog, just not well. Or you can have a zest for your Life, and really create all you want while enjoying it!

Yes, of course, you're going to stay in balance. How many times, though, have you found yourself saying, "well, it sounds fun, but I really *should* do ..." (something else more responsible, unimportant, boring and habitual)? You know by now to throw out the shoulds, to check in with yourself intuitively, to honor the areas of your life that need balance, and now to shake it up a little bit in order to gain new perspectives and hope in life.

So do shake it up! Look for opportunities to expand your horizons. Put the telephone to your right ear instead of your left (or vice versa) to have a conversation once. Write with your opposite hand once, and laugh at you while you do it! Walk backwards, hop, skip and jump! Use your whole body, your whole self.

Put some zest back in your life! It will surprise others as well as you, and if you've been feeling stuck, you will begin to see the possibilities of what life might hold for you. Whatever it is you choose to do, remember that you're giving up this moment to do it. Do it joyfully, do it completely, do it with zest, and sign your name to it!

BREATHE AND AFFIRM:

I FEEL THE ZEST FOR LIFE!

ZZZ's

Then, catch some ZZZ's! Sleep is so important. It is part of the balance we require as human beings. Rest for the physical body allows the mental and emotional bodies to settle, and to work well and in balance through the day. Often we get messages in our sleep. As you lie down to rest, know that you will wake up feeling rested and refreshed. Imagine the best possible day ahead of you, the one you have zest for, and let go and sleep! Then wake up and embrace the day!

Please find your own personal sleep pattern; the one that you awake feeling rested and refreshed from. Allow yourself enough sleep. Do you wake up without an alarm clock? When you have good and sufficient sleep, you will wake up naturally. Many people who live in areas with four seasons discover that their sleep patterns differ in summer and winter, with more or less sleep needed seasonally; this too is natural.

Is your thought pattern such that you believe you have to work too much to make time for sleep? Please remember that you can only do your best when you are well rested. The lack of sleep leads to many dis-eases in the body and soul. You may only need a few hours, or you may need 7 or 10 hours. Find your sleep balance, and know that the rest of your life will improve as you do.

As you live this life so that you do your very best, make it your intention to love, honor, trust and respect yourself so much that when you go to sleep, you do so feeling good about you and very, very light hearted.

BREATHE AND AFFIRM:

**I ALWAYS ALLOW MYSELF
GOOD SLEEP AND REST!**

PAMELA STORRS

Struck by lightning in Colorado, surviving a category 5 hurricane aboard a 47' sailboat in St. Croix, breaking and further damaging her back years later, being a bush pilot in Alaska at an early age, and a scuba diver in Hawaii and the Caribbean (and not in that order!) ... have simply served to enhance Pamela's unique perspective on our Life here on Earth, while the deceased continue to communicate with and through her.   Her newly revised book: ***BREATHE!! Your Life Depends On It!*** **A to Z Guide to Your Intuition** is the first primer on intuition, metaphysics, and the lifestyle that goes with it.

Psychic and Spiritual Advisor, Medium, Intuitive, Empath, Channel, Seer, Listener, Psychometrist, Medical Intuitive, Hypnotherapist, Past and Future Life Specialist, Dreamer/Visionary (also known as Clairvoyant, Clairsentient, Clairaudient, Clairalient, Claircognizant, a Healer, etc.), and generally Psychic since birth, Pamela has taught metaphysics, intuition, and meditation for more than 30 years.

She channels the Council of Light, who share information and guidance about the Shift, Earth, and our Consciousness. Pamela does Life Path Consultations and Life Path Coaching, and assists people in connecting with their loved ones on the other side. She has been a weekly radio guest and national media personality for many years, and consults for individuals and businesses, writes and speaks.

Visit www.PamelaStorrs.com for event information, appointments and rates, updates on her upcoming books and to book Pamela to speak to your organization. Opt in for email updates!

Made in the USA
Middletown, DE
25 June 2022

67778515R00176